GREEK RHETORIC BEFORE ARISTOTLE

Richard Leo Enos
Carnegie Mellon University

WAVELAND
PRESS, INC.
Prospect Heights, Illinois

Consulting Editor

Robert E. Denton, Jr.

For information about this book, write or call:
Waveland Press, Inc.
P.O. Box 400
Prospect Heights, Illinois 60070
(708) 634-0081

To Jessica and Susannah,
My two most recent daughters . . .

Acknowledgments

Undertaking this project would not have been possible without considerable help and cooperation. As an alumnus of the American School of Classical Studies at Athens, I have had opportunities to return to Greece and to gather evidence on rhetoric's early history. I have also been fortunate enough to enjoy the continued support and cooperation of the American School as well as the Greek Ministry of Culture and the Greek Archaeological Service, who generously granted permission to reproduce rare epigraphical sources central to this work. Appreciation is also extended to George Allen & Unwin, now Unwin Hyman of HarperCollins Publishers Limited of Great Britain, for permission to reproduce the map of Sicily from A. G. Woodhead's *The Greeks in the West*. Faber and Faber Ltd. was kind enough to grant permission to reproduce the map from L. R. Palmer's *The Greek Language*, and I thank them for their consideration. I also wish to acknowledge the generosity of Sage Publications for permitting me to use material I presented in *Oral and Written Communication: Historical Approaches* (1990), as well as Theresa Enos for material out of my essay in the Fall 1992 issue of *Rhetoric Review*. The author wishes to express appreciation to all parties for their efforts, particularly the international transactions of Richard Helppie.

I have also had the assistance of several libraries, including those at The University of Michigan, Indiana University, the American School of Classical Studies at Athens, Carnegie Mellon University, The University of Pittsburgh, and the Epigraphical Museum at Athens. The results of these efforts have enabled me to compile both primary sources and difficult-to-acquire secondary scholarship. This evidence, in the form of epigraphy, literary fragments, *scholia* (ancient commentary) and archaeological evidence, provides the source material for a much more specific rendering of the emergence of rhetoric as a discipline than our present anecdotal description permits. As mentioned above, the task of reconstructing this evidence is a monumental one, but my preliminary review, which includes archaeological and epigraphical reports of holdings at repositories, leads me to believe that this primary evidence will not only provide information on rhetoric's evolution as an art but also its place within a culture evolving from an oral to a literate society. Records from the Epigraphical Museum at Athens, for example, list inscriptions that bear directly on the political relationships between Athens and Sicily dealing with rhetoric. Additionally, literary and dramatic contests, with winners' names and cities of origin inscribed on stone monuments, offer another valuable source of information.

I also wish to acknowledge here support of a different sort, the kind that encourages and nurtures the research done at the centers mentioned above. First and foremost, I wish to acknowledge The National Endowment for the Humanities, whose generous stipend made this project possible. I am indebted to my family, colleagues and students for their encouragement and enthusiasm to continue my work. I particularly wish to thank Carnegie Mellon for their respect and support of humanistic studies in rhetoric. I also wish to thank my colleagues who are not only in the halls of my department but across the country, for they form a community whose nurturing is invaluable. I particularly wish to express my gratitude to two Jesuit associates, Fathers Walter Ong and the recently departed William Grimaldi, as well as my friends Janice Lauer, James L. Kinneavy and Edward P. J. Corbett and a special thanks to Wilbur Samuel Howell. I also wish to thank three of my kindest supporters, Dick Hayes, Karen Schriver, and Linda Flower who are never at a loss for a word of encouragement.

RLE

Contents

Preface

Popular accounts assert that rhetoric emerged as a discipline in the 5th Century B.C. in Greece. The attention it received from Plato and Aristotle, in addition to its malleable utility, assured its preservation for both the intellectually curious and the pragmatic. There is currently debate among historians of ancient rhetoric about the specific time that rhetoric was recognized as a discipline. Legend places that occurrence in Syracuse, Sicily and credits Corax and Tisias with its "founding" in 467 B.C.; others argue that rhetoric emerged as a discipline at a much later date (Schiappa 1991). Attempting to pinpoint a precise moment in history muddles the more important goal of understanding the processes that led to the establishment of rhetoric.

Rhetoric did not originate at a single moment in history. Rather, it was an evolving, developing consciousness about the relationship between thought and expression. This sensitivity about thinking, speaking and (later) writing happened in a variety of ways, at different times, and in a number of different areas of Greece. This awareness of the ancient Greeks resulted from what we now view as a variety of modes of expression and often because of factors that were not exclusively rational but frequently political, social and expedient. We do know that at some point ancient Greeks considered rhetoric to be a discipline, accepted it as a part of their education and — particularly in those cities that were governed by democracies — saw it as practical for the workings of their communities.

Both criticism and praise of rhetoric as a discipline centers on the subject of invention. That is, rhetoric offers systematic methods for creating artful and articulate discourse in both spoken and written forms. Aristotle focused on the ability to create proofs; reasoned discourse could be articulated in an effort to resolve situations that required popular judgment of opinion. Yet the "invention" of discourse is not limited solely to the creation of rational proofs. The task of this book is to illustrate the various types of discourse that developed in Greece and the methods used to refine them. An examination of these various approaches should provide a more expanded — and representative — view of the notion of invention. Such an understanding should help to sharpen our perspective on Plato's criticism of rhetoric, Aristotle's characterization of what rhetoric is (and ought to be), the nature and impact of the sophists, and the use of rhetoric in other genres.

There is one other point that is particularly important to note before reading this book. Current accounts of rhetoric in ancient Greece typically ignore the introduction of written composition to rhetoric or treat it as an after-thought, occurring long after systems of oral communication were firmly established. While there is no argument that speech preceded writing, this volume will make it clear that systems of written expression were in operation and shaping discourse before rhetoric emerged as a popular discipline. Moreover, it will also become apparent that the composition of Homeric literature and the evolution of prose writing through logography (written speech) were integral events in the development of rhetoric. We will see that as rhetoric became specialized into discrete functions — such as historical, legal, political, and ceremonial expression — systems of logography correspondingly moved to specialized modes of writing. Rhetoric became established and popular as a discipline because of the sophists of the fifth and fourth centuries B.C.; their presentation of rhetoric included both oral and written composition. In short, this book will make it apparent to the reader that oral and written systems of composition were in operation long before rhetoric was recognized as a discipline, that they inextricably evolved to establish rhetoric, and that their persistent unity helped secure its popular reception and perpetuation. To study the history of Greek rhetoric without recognizing the inherent relationship of oral and written composition produces an incomplete and imprecise understanding of the forces that developed rhetoric into a discipline.

Examining the confluence of the ideas and events which shaped rhetoric into a discipline is the purpose of this book. From this perspective, the Hellenic recognition of rhetoric as a discipline did not mark its beginning or origin but rather the consequence of a series of occurrences. The evolutionary process of rhetoric has frequently been discussed in broad terms, a generalized sweep of historic events preceding the emergence of rhetoric. Such an overview will happen indirectly, for major events and individuals will be discussed in order to provide a context for understanding topics under discussion. However, it is not the intent of this book to provide such a broad statement. If we are to have a sensitive understanding of the activities that foreshadowed rhetoric's emergence, it is imperative that we look closely at discrete occurrences and examine them in detail — particularly since they had such a profound impact on the way in which ancient Greeks viewed discourse and its creation. These events established paradigms about the relationship between thought and expression that created attitudes toward discourse which the ancient Greeks eventually assimilated into systems. Some of these paradigms reveal nascent sensitivity to self-created eloquence, others were shaped by the expediencies of the moment and still others by the influence of technologies such as writing. The rationality of rhetoric is the product of a number of these events, and presenting them in a coherent manner is the objective of this book. If this objective is attained, the reader should be able to begin the study of ancient rhetoric with a context that will promote a better understanding of rhetoric and its place in the societies of ancient Greece.

The bibliography at the end of this volume incorporates a considerable amount of scholarship in the history of rhetoric, particularly over the last few decades. Much of the work about the classical period of rhetoric has sought to refine, elaborate and adjust views of rhetoric that were formed over the last century. This fine tuning of ideas has come about by a closer reading of texts, such as Aristotle's *Rhetoric*, as well as a more substantial integration of standard sources. Some of the most notable contributions have been in general histories of rhetoric, which have helped to produce and to foster this resurgence of interest, particularly in the classical period. A greater sensitivity to social and cultural issues has also refined our ideas about classical rhetoric. As we learn more about the world of ancient Greeks and their worldview, we can posit more perceptive interpretations about their rhetoric. Scholarship over the last century has helped to advance this understanding in a number of ways: our sophistication over philological issues has increased, our understanding of Hellenic culture has likewise deepened, and our notion of the "history" of rhetoric has been more coherent and thorough than the patchwork accounts of our Victorian forefathers.

Yet, for all this scholarly advancement, there are still areas of need. Some of the more recent histories of rhetoric are not so much the result of newly discovered evidence but new perspectives for examining the same sources. While these perspectives are refreshing and often insightful, they do not in themselves provide new material for the study of ancient rhetoric. The attitudes about "doing history" also echo some of the predispositions of our forefathers. We tend — despite some re-orientations of characters and trends — to march through events in roughly the same fashion, forgetting that chronicles are not natural acts but only the perspectives of earlier historians which may or may not accurately reflect reality. Lastly, our work tends to start and finish at about the same time, and these parameters unconsciously set up boundaries that (by default) separate out other periods, topics, issues and individuals that do not fit the format.

This volume seeks to resolve some of these problems in a number of ways. The first is to provide a "pre-history" of classic rhetoric by examining emerging ideas that contributed to the establishment of rhetoric as a discipline in ancient Greece. Casting this project as a history, however, does not mean to impose an orderly flow of events where such order does not actually exist. To do so would be to tell a story at the expense of accuracy rather than represent events that do not always occur in a coherent pattern. Acts are not always causal or rational; forces of political preference, cultural desire and social norms also dictate ideas and systems of rhetoric. Second, much of the scholarship done in or about the origins of rhetoric is general and anecdotal. The effort here is to go into depth about important individuals, ideas and movements which will reveal forces shaping ideas about rhetoric and setting the agenda for what early Hellenic culture thought was (and was not) important about rhetoric — and the debates that naturally ensued because of these disagreements. The intent here, then, is not to provide broad, general overviews but rather specific instances that provoke a deeper understanding of phenomena. Lastly, this work will introduce sources that have not been examined, works that are known but typically not included in rhetoric's history and, consequently, new interpretations as well as the more traditional, literary ones.

This volume should provide the reader with an understanding of the multiplicity of forces that contributed to the shaping of rhetoric's history, as well as areas of inquiry that can and should continue to be examined. What is presented here as a pre-history is more accurately a preface to the history of rhetoric. As is true with any preface, carefully articulated preliminary statements are intended to provide the reader with a perspective that will maximize the benefits of the subsequent work. Certainly, in a general history of rhetoric many individuals would receive much greater attention. Although Protagoras' direct contributions to the development of rhetoric are still under discussion, there is little doubt that his contributions to philosophy and "linguistic developments" (Schiappa 198–203) warrant much more attention in a more generalized history. Similarly, the impact of Isocrates would also be a subject for discussion in a work that offered a broader range of topics. Here, however, our attention to prominent thinkers such as Protagoras and Isocrates focuses only on their impact on the evolving notions of discourse as they contribute to the emergence of rhetoric as a discipline. The object is to provide a context which will help readers better appreciate the more specialized studies of individuals as well as the broader, generalized histories. After reading this work, the reader should be able to turn to our current accounts of the history of classical rhetoric with new sources, new methods of analysis and criticism, and a better grounding for understanding and judgment.

Chapter I

Emerging Notions of Rhetoric
Homer, Hesiod and the Rhapsodes

The Homeric Mentality
and the Invention of Discourse

According to the eighth-century B.C. epic poet Hesiod (*Erga* 90–105), man lost his divine inspiration for eloquence when Pandora lifted the lid of the jar containing the gods' gifts to men. The righteousness of this act was justified as retribution for Prometheus's hubris in giving man the "technical" knowledge of fire. More importantly, the result of Zeus's revenge was that man had to rely on the creation of his own "techne" or art and replace eloquence with a rationally construed imitation of the divine act of effective expression. For Pietro Pucci, author of *Hesiod and the Language of Poetry*, "Pandora introduces the exclusivity of human language. She speaks only human language and, therefore is the first human who can no longer speak the language of the gods, of which Homer knows some words and to which Hesiod alludes in *Th*. 837" (91). Pucci's phrase, "of which Homer knows some words," is provocative for it hints at both the relationship and distinctions between god-breathed and human-created discourse.

To say that Homer's *Iliad* and *Odyssey* are paradigms in the history of literature is to utter a commonplace, but their contributions to the history and development of writing and rhetorical theory have received far less attention. Although preceding the canonization of rhetoric as a formal discipline by centuries, the composing techniques of Homer were admired by such famous

1

rhetoricians as Quintilian (10. 1. 46). However, they were pointedly contested by other ancient rhetoricians as appropriate for the study of rhetoric (Kennedy 1957, 23–35), principally because Homer predated rhetoric as a discipline and because Homeric discourse was thought to be a nonrational approach to expression. That is, those ancient rhetoricians who opposed using Homer as a model did so because Homeric compositions were thought to have been produced by the impulse of intuitive genius rather than the systematic study of the composition of discourse. This opposition to viewing Homer in relation to rhetoric in any way other than anecdotal is also shared by some contemporary rhetoricians. D. A. G. Hinks, in his essay "Tisias and Corax and the Invention of Rhetoric," claims that not only did the art or techne of rhetoric emerge in fifth-century B.C. Greece, but any examination prior to this period is "irrelevant to the proper history of rhetoric" (61). Yet, the composition of the *Iliad* and *Odyssey* has much to reveal about the epistemic development of rhetoric.

When the *Iliad* and *Odyssey* were composed in the latter half of the eighth-century B.C., Greece was in a twilight period of true oral literature. Although early Greeks rarely read silently — in fact it is virtually unheard of in Antiquity — the techniques of composing discourse exclusively for an oral medium were beginning to be replaced by developing scripts by the end of the seventh century B.C. (Kirk 1962, 314; Kirk 1965, 1–32; Stanford 1967, 1, n.4 ff.; Kennedy 1963, 4; Kirk 1976, 19–39). I. J. Gelb claims that "the development of a full Greek alphabet, expressing single sounds of language by means of consonant and vowel signs, is the last important step in the history of writing" (1974, 184). Gelb's emphasis, however, is on the development of sign-systems and in that sense, not much new has evolved in "the inner structural" development of writing (1974, 184). Yet, if we consider the notions of discourse evidenced in Homer's work and if we examine what the characters in the *Iliad* and *Odyssey* say and think about discourse, we may consider the *Iliad* and *Odyssey* the first important steps in the history of writing and rhetoric. This is a point which Otto Jespersen immediately establishes in his classic treatise, *Language: Its Nature, Development and Origin* (7), and one which has prompted other scholars of rhetoric's history (Kennedy 1957, 1975 and Murphy 1975) to recognize the possibility of such early beginnings.

In brief, even the earliest Greek writing indicates an emerging awareness of the relationship between human thought and the processes by which such thoughts and sentiments can be symbolically expressed. Three terms help to express the relationship between thought and expression: *heuristic, eristic* and *protreptic* discourse. Heuristic discourse is seen as a generative (helping to discover or learn) capacity to construe and apply some structuring of language. Heuristics has been a major concern not only of Aristotle's *Rhetoric* (Enos and Lauer 1992) but throughout the history of Greek rhetoric, as even a cursory reading of George Kennedy's *The Art of Persuasion in Greece* (e.g. 10) will reveal. The importance of this notion was clearly apparent to Latin rhetoricians, such as the unknown Roman author of the *Rhetorica Ad Herennium* (1. 3 ff) and Cicero (*De Inventione* ff.), both of whom labeled it *"inventio"* and gave it primacy among the canons of rhetoric. In fact, Kennedy's 1980 article in *Philosophy and Rhetoric* (185–189) demonstrates that the concept of heuristics was a central component to the Byzantine canons of rhetoric with Hermogenes' *On Invention* receiving great attention (see also Kustas 42 note). Eristic discourse is the advocacy for a particular point of view. The term "eristic" came to be synonymous with argumentative discourse and received commentary from both Plato (*Euthydemus* 272C; Lysis 211B) and Aristotle (*Rhetoric* 1371a, 1402a). Eristics was not only considered the "art of disputation" but was used to label philosophers of the Megarian school who were noted for their argumentative mode of discussion (Diogenes Laertius 2. 134). Plato eventually labelled the techne of eristic discourse as sophistry (*Sophista* 231E, 225C). Protreptic discourse is both directive and didactic but also associated with rational inquiry. Contrary to the notion of wrangling associated with eristics, protreptic discourse is seen as a didactic process whereby minds are "directed" for some instructive purpose (Skousgaard 379–380; Kustas 49, note). Protreptic discourse was strongly encouraged for philosophy by Plato (*Euthydemus* 278C,D; 288D,E; 282D) because it provides direction for thought leading to knowledge.

Plato characterized the instruction of sophists as misdirection. He believed that they taught eristic methods to subvert the truth in order to succeed at any cost, and thus had nothing to do with the more noble ends of protreptic discourse. Plato mercilessly lampooned sophists in his *Euthydemus* as not caring if they "talk nonsense" (288B, see also 277D,E; 278 B,C) and is very clear in his belief that speechwriters who do not know the distinct *technai* (techniques or skills) of generating and employing philosophical argument, or dialectic, will be severely constrained in their knowledge of the composing processes of discourse (*Euthydemus* 289 D,E). Their sophistic "art," Plato went on to say, is like a "wizard's art"; that is, sorcery "involves a wizard's charming venomous spiders and scorpions and other wild beasts and evil things," while sophistry "involves charming and persuading the ears of juries, assemblies and other mobs" (*Euthydemus* 289E, 290A). Plato's point clearly drives a wedge between the charm — and almost sensual enrapturement — of sophistic discourse and the philosophical inquiry toward knowledge characteristic of protreptic discourse. In brief, rhetoricians who engage in bantering, eristic argument only provide a "ridiculous display of their particular effort" and should be overlooked when seeking didactic discourse associated with protreptic procedures (*Euthydemus* 307B, see also 307A-C).

This chapter examines the dominant modes of Homeric discourse — heuristic, eristic and protreptic — and relates them to the notion of the divine "gift" of eloquence. This examination will show that conceptual processes of discourse synonymous with the formalization of rhetoric in the fifth century B.C. were already emerging three hundred years earlier. Awareness of the evolution of these conceptual processes will provide a more accurate understanding of both the history of rhetoric and an enriched understanding of the foundation of our discipline.

The concept of "heuristic" is present throughout the *Iliad* and *Odyssey* and is used to express some process of discovery. Homer freely uses the concept to indicate the discovery of persons, places, and gods (*Iliad* 5. 169; *Odyssey* 10. 252; *Iliad* 24. 98). Frequently this is done by an individual such as Athena "discovering" the proud suitors, or Odysseus "discovering" the house of Circe, or Hector "finding" Archeptolemus (*Odyssey* 10. 210; *Iliad* 8. 127). In this sense, an heuristic capacity which expresses the notion of discovering a physical event or entity does not discriminate between god or man. In fact, the notion of heuristics as discovered is refined to the extent that there is even a collective capacity to discover, such as in the statement "if we find a herd of oxen or a great flock," and personification as a lion would "discover" a deer or a wild goat (*Odyssey* 12. 300; *Iliad* 3. 24).

Homer also attributes a psychological capacity for heuristic discovery not confined to sensory awareness and uses the term "heuristic" to discuss the capacity of subjective self-awareness. Often, this discovery is in terms of projected emotive responses not associated with "rational" self-consciousness, such as "and they discovered Myrmidons delighting his heart with a clear-toned phorminx [lyre]" or Odysseus, who "discovered" himself sitting in the front hall of his home (*Iliad* 9. 185–186; *Odyssey* 14. 5). The use of "heuristic" in self-awareness and discovery is not limited to reflective self-consciousness. Homer often uses the term "heuristic" to indicate a potential capacity for joy or sorrow and even a concept of the negative as when they "did not find the gates boarded" (*Odyssey* 9. 535; *Odyssey* 13. 43; *Iliad* 12. 120–121). Evidence of the bridge between the physical and psychological sense of "heuristic" is evident in Homer's passage where the suitors "found the spirit of Achilles" in the sense of its representation as a physical form (*Odyssey* 24. 15).

All of the examples mentioned indicate mortal heuristic capacity for a range of power which extends from its use in the most physical sense to the most esoteric, futuristic modalities of subjective expression. This human techne for heuristics is central to understanding the inventive processes of the discovery and relationship of thought and discourse — that is, the human techne to discover and express complex thought and sentiments. Homer frequently discussed the power or human faculty of heuristics for discourse (*heuremena dunamai*) and several general modalities of heuristic processes are revealed (*Odyssey* 4. 374, 467; *Odyssey* 19. 157–158). Specifically, Homer discusses the human power to discover and contrive through words. Clearly evident is the idea of appropriate or suitable expression which can be "discovered." Nestor is characterized as being particularly sensitive to effective schemes for discourse and quick to point out shortcomings, as when he says, "For some time do we quarrel, nor do we have any capacity to discover any contrivance, for all our time here" (*Iliad* 2. 342–343). Nestor's criticism is a revealing one, for he expects his colleagues to demonstrate a faculty to discover some ability to devise a sign or technique through deliberation to resolve strife (*Odyssey* 12. 393; *Odyssey* 19. 157–158; *Iliad* 16. 472). Language is viewed as an awareness to discover a solution to a problem. This discovery process can not only occur collectively among individuals but even in a self-dialogue, as when Odysseus "took counsel with myself" so that he could invent a solution to outwit the Cyclops (*Odyssey* 9. 421–423).

There is a clear association in Homer with the notion of discovery and the translation of the findings into wily language. Odysseus, with his epithet of "many wiles" stands as an illustration of the human capacity to invent techniques to compose language.

Examples of his conniving abound throughout Book Nine of the *Odyssey* but particularly revealing is the passage when Odysseus tries to discover some way to "compose all sorts of cunning [plots] and contrivances" when trying to deceive the Cyclops Polyphemus (*Odyssey* 9. 421–423; see also, *Odyssey* 9. 19–20, 33). Odysseus is, in fact, lauded by Homer and proud of his ability to invent and compose devious discourse and is even told explicitly by his colleagues not to "conceal with crafty cunning what you really think but to speak up" (*Odyssey* 8. 548–549). The notion of inventional language as deception would be a central grounding for Gorgias' sophistic rhetoric. Here we see the notion of language as a deception of reality invented through human capacity centuries earlier in Homer (D-K 82. B11. 6, 8, 11, 14).

Homer's writing reveals a sensitivity to the human capacity to invent discourse and to compose or weave such language for effect. The modalities of this human capacity are present in two types of discourse, eristic and protreptic. The Homeric notion of eristic discourse is taken to be more than the mere symbolization of thought and sentiment but rather the inherent power of the language itself. Eris or strife is a personification and can be god-induced (*Iliad* 4. 440; *Iliad* 5. 518, 740; *Iliad* 11. 3, 73; *Iliad* 18. 535; *Iliad* 20. 48. *Odyssey* 3. 136, 161). It can also come into being as a result of discord or disagreement, particularly when induced by wine (*Iliad* 20. 55. *Odyssey* 6. 92; *Odyssey* 3. 136; *Odyssey* 20. 267; *Odyssey* 19. 11). It is the human power to create strife through discourse which is particularly revealing here because Homer cojoins the notion of eristics with wrangling. The association of "strife and wrangling" occurs so frequently in Homer that it can almost be classified as formulaic (*Iliad* 2. 376; *Odyssey* 20. 267). According to Ben Edwin Perry, the frequency of such coordinating notions is not only characteristic of Homeric language but is a paratactic structure encouraging the "spontaneous absorption" of notions through a "strung-along style" (410–418, especially 412).

The relationship of "strife and wrangling" is important to understand. Homer often combined strife and wrangling. On some occasions, strife provoked wrangling, while in other instances, the opposite happened. Yet, just as Greeks later bonded concepts of the true *and* the beautiful together, so also did Homer equate strife and wrangling. This co-existence of strife and wrangling forged a unity of reciprocal relationships. Strife, particularly when mixed with wine, induced wrangling, but wrangling also produced strife, as when Athena characterizes taunting words as a "reproachful attack," or when the suitors are told to "restrain your spirit from rebuke and blows, so that no strife or wrangling may appear"and they all "bit their lips "(*Iliad* 1. 210–211; *Odyssey* 20. 266–268). In such moments of passion "winged words" are sent to the gods so that no violence can be caused when one is "burning on fire" with rage (*Iliad* 21. 359–361, 368; see also, *Odyssey* 2. 269). For Homer, the concept of wrangling holds no great esteem; in fact, his clearest view of the term is when he has Aeneas say, "to forcibly quarrel with strife and wrangling between us" is "like women who engage in bitter wrangling" (*Iliad* 20. 251–255). While such lowly prattle has no place in a Homeric man's world, it is clear that manly argument rarely occurs in a climate of quiet, dispassioned reason. In fact, Telemachus tells his own mother the queen that, despite her well-reasoned views, it is not her function but his — and that of men in general — to be the spokesperson of the home (*Odyssey* 1. 356–359).

For Homer, the eristic power of language is bounded with emotion and the possibility of violence. The clearest association with "strife and wrangling" is that violent thoughts lead to violent words and, eventually, violent deeds. Individuals are often told to curb their violent words so that strife and wrangling do not lead to blows (*Iliad* 1. 210; *Odyssey* 19. 11; *Odyssey* 18. 13; *Odyssey* 20. 266–267). Conversely, strife would continue if not for the power of words to thwart it as when Homer writes that "strife would have [protrepticly] gone forward . . . had not Achilles spoken" (*Iliad* 23. 490–491). In brief, man has the power to generate strife though discourse, as do gods. Man has the power to resolve strife through discourse, as do gods. Man, like the gods, has the capacity to generate discourse which will create and mitigate violent words and create and mitigate violent acts of "strife and wrangling." Words can sting or be sweet and their power is often seen in terms of emotive and sensory responses, as when Odysseus says, "your speech has bit my heart" (*Iliad* 1. 247–249; see also *Odyssey* 8. 183–185). To this point we can see that Homeric characters had some concept of an inventional capacity to generate discourse but that this self-consciousness of their "heuristic" capacity produced discourse which was eristic, or emotive-based as well as emotive-directed, by arousing some sort of attitudinal disposition. Odysseus frequently mentions that an individual could or could not "persuade the heart within my breast" (*Odyssey* 9. 33).

Yet, discourse can have the capacity to check a "strong-hearted spirit" and induce "kindliness" (*Iliad* 9. 255–256). Words can have the capacity to "turn" or direct human thought (*Odyssey* 11. 18; 12. 381) in a way approaching rationalism rather than in strictly sensual terms, which leads to the Homeric notion of protreptic (instructionally directive) discourse. We know that when rhetoric was established as a formal discipline it not only gave treatment to *ethos* and *pathos* but also to *logos*, the rational capacity to persuade other minds (Aristotle, *Rhetorica* 1356a). Certainly, any position which argues for an emerging notion of rhetoric must inquire into the human capacity to structure discourse toward the "reasonable." There is, in fact, evidence to indicate that notions of reasonable discourse are to be found in Homer.

As indicated earlier, Plato strongly opposed sophists who practiced eristic discourse but would not engage in the rational didactic techniques of protreptic discourse (*Euthydemus* 288B-D, 272B-C, 289E, 290A, 278C,D). We know from Pucci, that Hesiod had discussed the concept of false and true discourse, which he called respectively "crooked" and "straight" (45–49). Homer also has a directional concept of protreptic discourse and refers to yielding or betaking oneself willingly to do something (*Iliad* 5. 700; *Iliad* 6. 336). Moreover, there is present in Homer the notion of a human capacity to generate "gentle" words to sooth the mind. Perhaps the most sensitive illustration of this phenomenon of protreptic discourse occurs in the *Iliad* when Alexander says "I had a desire to direct my [thought] to sadness. And even now my wife sought to persuade me with gentle words" (*Iliad* 6. 336–338). It is fitting that women, who are unfairly portrayed as having nothing whatsoever to do with the real power of discourse beyond "wrangling," are used to illustrate a capacity for rationality in time of stress.

Although the human heuristic capacity to discover discourse is evident in Homer as well as the potential to manufacture powerful eristic and reasonable protreptic discourse, it should not be forgotten that these are emerging, and even primitive, notions of discourse. To appreciate this perspective, we should reflect on the ability to produce genuine eloquence. There is little doubt that in Homer eloquence is god-produced and god-given. As is evidenced in Hesiod's account of Pandora, Zeus gave, and later took away, divine speech (*Erga* 90–105; Friedrich Solmsen 1954). Yet, to say that Zeus completely took away divine speech would be imprecise and not account for Hesiod's statement that both he and Homer knew "a few" divine words (*Theogenia* 837; Pucci, 91). Despite man's limitations to struggle with the development of his own techne, there is evidence of what E. R. Dodds calls "psychic intervention" (5). Individuals who are eloquent are seen as having a gift from the gods and themselves are "god-like" (Homer, *Odyssey* 8. 165–185).

This divine gift from the gods is reserved for two categories of humans. The first group is royal or god-descended and god-blessed. Nestor, the King of Pylos, is the model of eloquence in Homer (*Iliad* 1. 247–249). Yet, Odysseus, the King of Ithaka, is viewed not only as wily but eloquent, as is indicated in the *Iliad* when Homer says, "But when he [Odysseus] put forth his great voice from his breast, as like a snow storm in the winter, then indeed could no mortal man quarrel with Odysseus and then indeed did we wonder to behold his image" (*Iliad* 3. 221–224). Lastly, the "hero" of the *Iliad*, Achilles, is not only god-born but has been raised in a kingly fashion so that he can be "a rhetor of speech and a doer of deeds" (*Iliad* 9. 443). Of great importance here is the use of the term *rhetor*, for it is the earliest and only known instance in which the term is used by Homer throughout the entire *Iliad* and *Odyssey*. It is a provocative point to historians of rhetoric that this earliest notion of the term which would be the basis for the founding of the discipline of rhetoric centuries later is now clearly associated with the god-blessed hero Achilles.

The other group of individuals in the *Iliad* and *Odyssey* who have the capacity for eloquence are the *aoidoi*, the bards who "weave" together or compose chants of heroic tales to honor the gods. Demodocus and Phemius are two examples from the *Odyssey* (1. 154; 8. 65–67; 13. 27–28). Aoidoi are invariably given the epithet "divine" or "god-like" aoidoi who receive their power of eloquence from Zeus (*Odyssey* 1. 325–349; *Odyssey* 8. 43, 47, 87, 539; *Odyssey*, 13. 27; *Odyssey* 9. 3,4). The sixth century B.C. lyric poet Pindar considered "*aoidoi*" to be "weavers of chants" (*Nemean Odes* 2. 1, 2). These composers of discourse were the pioneers of the techniques of oral literature and evolved into the formal guild of rhapsodes who are discussed in Plato's *Ion*. Both the aoidoi, and their later descendants the rhapsodes, orally composed and preserved texts of heroic tales, of which the *Iliad* and *Odyssey* are the most famous. During the sixth century B.C., the rhapsodes developed written compositional techniques to preserve by script the collection of Homeric words and grammar which was becoming increasingly rare and, consequently, difficult to pronounce. These compositional techniques became so established that by the fifth century B.C. private texts of Homer were known to have existed in Athens (Xenophon *Symposium* 3.6; *Memorabilia* 4. 2. 10).

In review, this section addressed several issues. First, the earliest Greek literature known indicates that there was an awareness among the characters of the *Iliad* and *Odyssey* of heuristic processes which could be used to develop human technai to produce discourse. Secondly, this discourse had power. The power was man-made, but it could produce emotive effects and resolve discord and strife through conceptual, eristic discourse. Third, there is some evidence that a more gentle structuring of discourse to turn or direct the mind and sooth emotions was the precursor to protreptic discourse. Lastly, man has some potential to be eloquent but the gift was god-given inspiration and available to only a chosen few. Although women could wrangle and produce strife, they could not be eloquent or even wily in their discourse; they had to content themselves with being reasonable!

The implications of these points are important for the history of rhetoric. It is clear by Homer's tales of a proto-literate, Bronze Age culture that conceptual processes were being formulated for the structuring and understanding of discourse. There is an awareness of the potential of this power and even an indication of the relationship of thought and discourse. Even at this early stage of development, human technai for the structuring of discourse were being developed. More importantly, with this consciousness there is an emerging shift from a theocentric notion to more of an anthropocentric notion of discourse. The supremacy of the gods as the generating force of effective expression would be challenged to the extent that words and arguments could be composed by sophists so powerful that they could defy the very existence of the gods who had once been credited with giving them the divine power of speech. To Zeus, it may have been better if Pandora had not opened the lid of that jar in the first place.

The Evolution of the Hellenic Rhapsode

A good song, I think. The end's good—that came to me in one piece—and the rest will do. The boy will need to write it, I suppose, as well as hear it. Trusting to the pen; a disgrace, and he with his own name made. But write he will, never keep it in the place between his ears. And even then he won't get it right alone. I still do better after one hearing of something new than

he can after three. I doubt he'd keep even his own songs for long,
if he didn't write them. So what can I do, unless I'm to be
remembered only by what's carved in marble?
(Opening passage of Simonides in *The Praise Singer* by Mary
Renault).

Traditionally, Corax and Tisias of Sicily (fifth century B.C.) are
acknowledged as the inventors of rhetoric. However, rhapsodes
were developing techniques for the theory and practice of oral
literature at least three centuries earlier and were a link between
Homer and the systematized rhetoric that emerged centuries later
in classical Athens. Milman Parry's discovery that the *Iliad* and
Odyssey were oral documents was an extremely important
contribution to the study of the prehistory of rhetoric. Parry's
exhaustive efforts and evidence clearly reveal that Homeric
compositions were recorded so that they could be recited aloud
(Milman Parry; Adam Parry 1–50; Dodds 1968; cf. Davidson
216–218, 224). The implications of this discovery not only indicate
a shared interest in oral technique between rhapsodes (the
individuals largely responsible for the transmission of Homeric
literature) and ancient rhetoricians but also compel an examination
of the role of rhapsodes in codifying, transmitting, and even
composing this oral literature. More importantly, research done by
Parry, Albert B. Lord, and Berkley Peabody demonstrates that early
oral compositions reveal an ancient oral tradition functioning as a
"highly sophisticated socio-linguistic institution that plays a central
role in maintaining the continuities of the culture in which it
occurs" (Peabody 1). Rhapsodes were composers of epic poetry who
continued from the formation of Homeric literature through the
evolution of rhetoric into a discipline. Yet the relationship between
the rhapsodes and the development of rhetoric was far from
autonomous. In the period prior to rhetoric's emergence as a
discipline, rhapsodes developed compositional techniques that laid
a foundation which contributed to rhetoric's development.

Some of the more valuable contributions about rhapsodes came
from the German philologist Harald Patzer (1952), who made
commendable efforts to explain the etymology and nature of the
term "rhapsode" (ῥαψῳδός), and Carlo Odo Pavese (1974), who
made a thorough study of the epic tradition of rhapsodic literature.
Both Patzer and Pavese, however, concentrated on linguistic issues
of composition and not on the evolution of the tradition itself. In
the field of speech communication, Eugene and Margaret Bahn

(1932, 1970) deserve recognition for calling attention to the importance of rhapsodes in the development of Greek literature. Donald E. Hargis (1970) improved on the efforts of the Bahns by synthesizing and focusing earlier research.

Despite these efforts, contemporary research on the origin and role of rhapsodes, particularly prior to and during the establishment of rhetorical theory, is slight. Moreover, several incompatible notions about rhapsodes persist in the few studies that have been conducted. First, the origin and development of a rhapsodic tradition is unclear. Likewise, the relationship between a group of Homeric experts, called "Homeridae" (e.g. Pindar *Nemean Odes* 2. 1, 2), and rhapsodes has not been thoroughly explained. Second, the importance of rhapsodes to the history of Greek literature is still an issue of dispute. Writers such as G.S. Kirk regard rhapsodes as "decadent and moribund" entertainers who were guilty of "straining" for "rhetorical effects" which corrupted the text of Homer (Kirk 1965, 29). Eugene and Margaret Bahn do imply that rhapsodes played significant roles in the development of Greek thought, but they do not specify either the nature or impact of such a role (13). Finally, there is no agreement concerning the date of the demise of rhapsodes nor why it occurred. Hargis, for example, argues that rhapsodes reached their zenith at the time of Plato but persisted until the time of Christ (397). Martin Litchfield West claims that rhapsodes practiced their art down to the third century after Christ (*OCD* 920). This chapter attempts to resolve the uncertainties noted above by tracing the development of a rhapsodic tradition prior to and throughout the period of Hellenic classical rhetoric.

Etymological Issues Concerning the Homeric "Rhapsode"

As the preceding chapter reveals, a casual reading of the *Iliad* and the *Odyssey* inaccurately suggests that such characters as Phemius and Demodocus could be stereotyped as illiterate improvisors chanting Homeric verse. If ancient terminology is properly understood, however, these predecessors to rhapsodes were developing and employing systems of oral discourse even before the Homeric age. The origin and relationship of Homeric interpreters with rhapsodes, moreover, is best understood through etymology, for the literal meaning of such terms as "bard" and "rhapsode" has been a source of misunderstanding. The term "bard" is particularly confusing, since it has no Greek equivalent and implies a distinction from the term "rhapsode" which is essentially arbitrary. The closest cognate to a "bard" is the Latin *bardus*, which means a poet, singer or minstrel (usually in reference to Gauls). Individuals such as Phemius and Demodocus, who are commonly labeled by translators as "bards" or "minstrels," are consistently called "aoidoi" (ἀοιδοί) in Homeric literature. Yet Plato, who lived over three centuries after Homer, specifically refers to Phemius in the *Ion* as a "rhapsode" (*Ion* 533C). Plato would seem to be mistaken, for he should have called Phemius an "aoidos," as did Homer. What Plato was doing, however, was substituting a contemporary Attic Greek term for an outdated Homeric Greek term and providing an important clue to the development of the term "rhapsode" and an indication of the need to examine its Homeric origin.

In Homeric literature, an aoidos could represent any entertainer who chanted out a tale and who often kept rhythm with a lyre or staff. Both Homer and Hesiod provide several examples throughout their works (Homer, *Iliad* 9. 186–189; *Odyssey* 8. 65–67, 105, 254, 261–262; 13. 28–30; 17. 260–263; 22. 330–333. Hesiod, *Theogonia* 29–32). In fact, the primary distinction of an aoidos from a musician seems to be only that the accompaniment is secondary to the oral work. Hesiod, for instance, distinguished an "*aoidos*" from an individual who specialized or limited himself only to playing an instrument such as the kithara (Hesiod, *Incertae Sedes Fragmenta* 1; Diogenes Laertius 8. 1. 25). In ancient lyric poetry, the common practice was for the aoidos to accompany his lays to a musical beat; virtually every form of Greek poetry was associated with music (Plato, *Ion* 530A; *OCD* 705). When translators arbitrarily distinguish among the Homeric bard, minstrel, and rhapsode, they obscure the unity which enabled an individual to blend song, music and poetry. Moreover, to impose the notion of specialization is to imply a refinement which had not yet occurred. Initially, Homeric aoidoi such as Phemius did not credit their oral ability to any systematic technique, as did later rhapsodes such as *Ion*. Rather, as E.R. Dodds indicates, they attributed their ability to the "psychic intervention" of divine inspiration (10–11). In brief, it would be more precise to consider these Homeric chanters as "pre-rhapsodes"; we should qualify the meaning within the context rather than obscure what is essentially the same phenomenon with various labels. There is little doubt, however, that rhapsodes eventually took on a very specialized role as interpreters of Homeric literature, but such distinctions cannot reasonably be drawn in the Homeric age.

Even ancient scholars were in a quandary over the etymology of the term "rhapsode." This uncertainty is illustrated in the writings of the second century B.C. grammarian Dionysius Thrax: "Rhapsody is the aspect of poetry embracing some proposed subject. Moreover, rhapsody is [derived] from the [term] 'rod,' from the fact that men traveled around with a bay-wood rod singing the poems of Homer" (Τέχνη γραμματική 5; see also, Pfeiffer, 269). For Dionysius, the meaning of rhapsody (ραψωδια) is derived from two words: "rod" (ῥάβδos), and "chant" (ᾠδή). Hence, for Dionysius, the term "rhapsode" came from the combined term "rod-chanter," one who beats out the metre of his chant with a staff. This interpretation is supported by archaeological evidence, for among the British Museum collection of Greek pottery is an early fifth century B.C. Attic red-figure amphora (E. 27) which shows a rhapsode with a staff (ῥάβδos) chanting a poem (Kirk 1962, plate 76; Callimachus, *Fragmenta* 138 ([5]Fr. 3. 10 P.); cf. Pausanius 9. 30. 3).

Although Dionysius' interpretation differs from the concept of rhapsodes as "weavers of chants," its etymology is not incompatible with the earlier explanations of Hesiod and Pindar, both of whom were closer in time to the Homeric age than was Dionysius (Hesiod, *Fragmenta Dubia* 3; scholia on Pindar, *Nemean Odes* 2. 1, 2). In fact, annotators of Dionysius' writing posit both of the above interpretations: early rhapsodes not only wove together swatches of heroic verse but often used a staff or lyre for rhythmic accompaniment (5, accompanying scholia 8, 9). Pindar even used a term for rod (ῥάβδos, see below) in a metaphorical sense to indicate the "standard" for measuring verse, and Homer indicated that divine inspiration (μένos) could be transmitted through a staff (*Isthmian Odes* 4. 36–39). In the Homeric sense, a "ῥάβδos" is usually taken to be a sort of magic wand, such as those used by Circe, Athena and Hermes (*Iliad* 13. 59 ff.; 24. 343. *Odyssey* 10. 238, 319; 16. 172; E. R. Dodds p, n. 52).

Etymological perspectives from such ancient authors as Dionysius Thrax provide important information for the interpretation of oral literature. With these terms in mind, Homer may be considered the father of rhapsodes, for he was the first known aoidos to present a formal codification and canonization of heroic oral literature. The Homeric term "aoidos" first became associated with a conscious, rational system of oral discourse when, in the eighth century B.C., Hesiod called himself and Homer "ἀοιδόι" who weave their compositions together (ῥάψατες ἀοιδήν) in order to compose (Hesiod *Fragmenta Dubia* 3; scholia on Pindar *Nemean Odes* 2. 1, 2). Evidence cited above indicates that aoidoi such as Homer and Hesiod were the first Hellenic thinkers to advance formalized systems for both presenting and understanding oral literature—an activity which ought to be recognized as contributing to the evolution of rhetoric as a discipline.

The Stabilization of the Rhapsodic Tradition

Two factors marked the rhapsodic tradition: the modification of the Greek language and the introduction of written literature. The Phoenician alphabet was introduced in Greece as early as the thirteenth century B.C., but the earliest extant "literature" is from the eighth century B.C. and was used as an aid in storytelling (Ullman 22; Kirk 1965, 10; Pfeiffer 269; Kirk 1976, 19–39). Although types of script called Linear B and Linear A existed during the Bronze Age, Greece lapsed back into a pre-literate level by the eleventh century B.C. and lost the art of writing for several centuries. During this pre-literate dark age, storytellers chanted heroic adventures similar to those in Homer but preserved and conveyed their tales orally. Homer thus wrote about other aoidoi like Demodocus and Phemius, who lived during the oral, preliterate period.

Throughout the rise of Greek literature, the works of Homer maintained their popularity. The desire of listeners to hear the ancient, correct pronunciation of Homer's works also endured—despite the influence of several dialects and foreign languages (Pfeiffer 11). Classical Greeks saw writing as a means to facilitate oral communication, and the fifth-century B.C. pre-socratic philosopher Kritias even claimed that the "Phoenicians invented writing as an aid to speaking (Kritias, D-K 88. B2). This is a point of no small significance, for as the rest of the language went through the natural process of simplifying its structure, numerous Homeric terms became increasingly rare and obsolete (γλῶσσαι) and needed to be recorded so that their "proper" meaning and pronunciation would be insured for future listeners. Consequently, an ever-widening gap emerged between the fixed language preserved in the works of Homer and the constantly changing Greek tongue.

Despite the linguistic changes that took place in the Greek language from the eighth to the fourth centuries B.C. (Maas 1), the desire to preserve the euphony of the Homeric tongue encouraged individual rhapsodes to record, and thus preserve, the almost sacrosanct interpretation (Plato *Ion* 530C,D ff.; Pfeiffer 10–11). Pindar claimed that even in his time audiences required individuals who could explain and preserve literature (*Olympian Odes* 2. 83–85; *Pythian Odes* 1. 93–94; *Isthmian Odes* 7. 16–19). In the twilight of this oral, pre-literate period, Homeric interpreters relied strongly on memory, and their reputation for reciting entire sections of Homer was widespread (Pindar *Nemean Odes* 7. 14–16; *Isthmian Odes* 6. 98–110; Plato *Ion* 537A,B). Rudolf Pfeiffer argues that there is "no evidence for book production on a large scale, for the circulation of copies, or for a reading public in the lyric age. The power of memory was unchallenged, and the tradition of poetry and early philosophy remained oral" (25). Even the term rhapsody, in its earliest sense, came to mean the chanting of an entire book of Homer — or about five hundred lines at a single session (Liddell and Scott 1566, col. 2; Kirk 1962, 306–307, n. 2). In this respect, the *Iliad* and *Odyssey* are actually stories woven together with formulaic transitions. Moreover, the emergence of writing facilitated attempts to preserve Homeric literature and pronunciation, for interpreters were able to use texts or copies of passages to aid their memories.

The efforts to stabilize the Homeric tongue, particularly through writing, enable us to view rhapsodes with more precision. During the purely oral period, aoidoi entertained listeners and related heroic stories. with an emphasis on creative improvisation as well as the transmission of familiar stories. Rhapsodes began to appear during the literate period. Herodotus was the first known writer of the fifth-century B.C. to use the term rhapsode (ῥαψῳσούς), an individual who chanted Homeric poems a (5. 67; cf. Sophocles *Oedipus Tyrannus* 391). Thus, somewhere between the late sixth and early fifth centuries B.C. the term came into common usage. By the late fifth and early fourth centuries B.C. of Plato's Athens, it meant a professional interpreter who recited almost exclusively the works of Homer (Plato *Ion* 530C; *Leges* 658B). In fact, a work in the corpus of *Homerica*, which is dated as early as the fourth century B.C., even refers to Homer as a "ῥαψῳδούτα" or "sort of rhapsode" ([*Homerica*], *Of the Origin of Homer and Hesiod, and Their Contest* 315; Hesiod *Fragmenta Dubia* 3; Plato *Leges* 658B).). In brief, G.S. Kirk claims that somewhere between 625–575 B.C. there was a "progressive eclipse of the aoidos with his *kitharis* [κίθαρις] and the firm establishment of the trained reciter, the rhapsode" (Kirk

1965, 314; cf. Hayman 150; Patzer 324). During the seventh and sixth centuries B.C. the alphabet and writing became more pervasive; appreciation for literature became more widespread; the *Iliad* and *Odyssey* were popular, but the pronunciation of Homeric Greek was virtually lost. At this time, rhapsodes began to establish themselves as professionals who not only claimed expertise as Homeric scholars but also as Homeric philologists and phoneticians who functioned as linguistic "guardians" of Homeric pronunciation.

Although the specific time during which the evolution from aoidos to rhapsode occurred is uncertain, there can be little doubt that the change from a preliterate to a literate Hellenic culture was a dominant force influencing the development of a rhapsodic tradition. Prior to the eighth and seventh centuries B.C., individuals relied upon their memories as the primary means for transmitting literature. Even a cursory reading of the *Iliad* and *Odyssey* reveals numerous formulae that were mnemonic aids in recalling passages. With the emergence of writing, however, rhapsodes began to construct texts of Homeric literature to aid their oral presentations (Xenophon *Memorabilia* 4. 2. 10; *Symposium* 3. 6). A series of passages cited from ancient sources which support the notion of writing being used to aid memory can be found in Pfeiffer (26). Frederic George Kenyon and Colin Henderson Roberts explain: "Long after poems and other literary works were written down as a matter of course, the normal method of publication was oral. Books were essentially *aides-mémoire* for the author or performer, not a primary means of communication to an audience. This view of the book as a *hypomnema* or substitute for recital persists until Plato, if not later" (*OCD* 173). Similarly, George Miller Calhoun offers a very informative presentation on the relationship between oral and written litigation (177–93).

Rhapsodes played an important part in the development of oral and written expression, for their texts of Homer not only facilitated memory but also codified and thus stabilized the literature (Kirk 1962, 309). Clearly, divergent copies existed, and corrected copies were undoubtedly numerous. During the dawning of the literary period, rhapsodes shifted from preliterate improvisors to experts at codifying, preserving, and orally interpreting *Homerica* for listeners. Athens became the leader in book-trade, but up to the sixth century B.C. no single authoritative text was compiled. On the contrary, considerable confusion must have resulted because of the numerous swatches and variant rhapsodic texts which existed (Pfeiffer 25). To resolve this confusion, a single text presenting the "entire" *Iliad* and *Odyssey* was needed and the rhapsodes played a leading role in this ambitious project.

The opportunity for rhapsodes to canonize Homer's works came in the sixth century B.C. during a Panathenaic contest under Pisistratus. Contests were an integral aspect of Greek life; they included athletic events as well as cultural performances. At the Pythian Games, for example, crowds of musicians actively competed for honors alongside athletes. These festivals, which were centered around religious themes, were a natural arena in which rhapsodes practiced their art. By the eighth century B.C., the concept of panhellenic festivals drew competitors from major Greek states (Pfeiffer 5). Hellenic interest in art and athletics may account for the frequency of such contests (Isocrates, *Panegyricus* 43–46), and the deference which all Greeks shared toward the *Iliad* and *Odyssey* offered a universal bond.

Until the sixth century B.C., there was not a suitable panhellenic text which could function as a standard, authorized copy. By this time, Homeric readings were a recognized part of Panathenaic festivals (Kirk 1962, 302–3). In an attempt to resolve textual difficulties, the Athenian tyrant Pisistratus ordered the scattered readings of Homeric literature to be collected and assembled. The orator Lycurgus adds support to the contention that rhapsodes were individuals chosen to stabilize the works of Homer when he said to the Athenians: "Your fathers held the poet [Homer] in such regard that they established a law so that at every five-yearly Panathenaea his epic works alone, of all the poets, would be chanted by the rhapsodes" (*Contra Leocratem* 102). Plato argues that Hipparchus, not Pisistratus, ordered the canonization of the *Iliad* and *Odyssey* by rhapsodes (*Hipparchus* 228B) while Diogenes Laertius (1. 57) claims that the codification took place under Solon, a position supported by Hayman (144). T. W. Allen argues for a different date and locale for the canonization of Homer's works but does not attack ancient references which credit rhapsodes for their efforts (40, 48–49). Lastly, Josephus reinforced the testimony of Lycurgus by claiming that up to the time of Pisistratus such works were transmitted only orally (*Contra Apionem* 1. 12).

While it is clear that arguments about locale, time and authority exist concerning the literate standardization of the *Iliad* and *Odyssey*, there is no disagreement that the rhapsodes were the composers and consequently the sources for literate compositional techniques and form. The construction of a standardized Homeric text may have meant that one rhapsode had to begin his interpretation where the preceding rhapsode had finished; the process continued until the entire work was completed. Whether this phenomenon, called the "Pisistratean recension," actually took place during the rule of Pisistratus has been contested (Kirk 1962, 312, 317; Pfeiffer 6, 7). By the fifth century B.C., private texts of Homer were not uncommon and rhapsodes who knew Homer by heart were common in Athens (Xenophon *Symposium* 3. 6; *Memorabilia* 4. 2. 10).

With the codification of the *Iliad* and *Odyssey* came the formation of the *Homeridae*, the most prestigious members of the rhapsodic guild who may well have functioned as judges in interpretative contests (Plato *Ion* 530D; Hargis 1977, 1–12). The exact date the Homeridae guild was formed and their relationship to rhapsodes in general has neither been thoroughly examined nor completely understood (*OCD* 526). Homeridae prospered on the island of Chios, the legendary birthplace of Homer, and claimed to be his descendants (*OCD* 526). The reference to Homeridae as types of rhapsodes is made by Pindar, who describes these "sons of Homer" as "weavers of chants" (*Nemean Odes* 2. 1, 2; [Plutarch] *Homeri Vita* 2. 2). In scholia referring to Pindar (*Nemean Odes* 2. 1, 2) Athenaeus (22B) indicates that the most famous of these Homeridae at his time was Cynaethus of Chios, who flourished about 504 B.C..

The influence of the Homeridae spread as rhapsodes such as Xenophanes of Colophron (b. 570 B.C.) traveled throughout Greece reciting his own poetry and critiquing both Homer and Hesiod (D-K 21. A1). Theagenes of Rhegium (fl. c. 525 B.C.) was the author of *On Homer*. In it, he argued that the gods of Homeric literature were actually personifications of natural elements and abstract entities. His interpretation of Homer included comments on linguistics as well as literary and grammatical criticism (D-K 8. 2, 1, 1a; Pfeiffer 10–11). Although Theagenes cannot be considered one of the Homeridae with absolute certainty, there is little doubt that he represents the essence of rhapsodic scholarship—that is, an interpreter of both literary meaning and linguistic accuracy. Eventually, rhapsodes other than those who came from Chios were admitted to the Homeric guild, and by Plato's time Homeridae were highly esteemed throughout Athens (Ion 530D; *Phaedrus* 252B). In short, Homeridae were a distinguished guild of itinerant rhapsodes who consciously attempted to illuminate meaning in Homer and to preserve written collections of words which were becoming increasingly rare, obsolete, and therefore difficult to pronounce (Pfeiffer 12; Aristotle *Poetica* 1459a9 ff.; Isocrates *Helen* 65).

The recognition rhapsodes had received under Pisistratus continued. As festivals and games gained popularity, so did the contests for rhapsodes. Musicians and poets, who shared honors equally with athletes, were encouraged to compete at the Pythian, Nemean, Isthmian, and Olympian games — as Pindar's lyric poems reveal. As the intellectual center for the Hellenic world, Athens also encouraged rhapsodes to participate in her contests. Pericles established by decree not only a general contest for music and poetry, but also an odeion, or concert/lecture hall, to house such displays (Plutarch *Vita Parallelae: Pericles* 13; Pausanias 1. 8. 6 and 7. 20. 6; Philostratus *Vita Sophistarum* 571, 579). By Plato's time, rhapsodic contests at the Panathenaea held great prestige. Plato's dialogue-character *Ion* proudly referred to his competition in the event (*Ion* 530B; *Leges* 658B). By Plato's time, rhapsodes commonly dressed in conspicuous apparel and declaimed from a dias (*Ion* 530B, 535D,E). Contrary to Plato's implications, respect for rhapsodes was widespread, particularly among sophists such as Protagoras, who admired rhapsodes for their attempts to use Homer as a means of providing a practical education (D-K 80. A5; Plato *Protagoras* 317B; Pfeiffer 16).

Over the centuries, rhapsodes continued to evolve into a professional guild of individuals who were not only educators in Homeric oratory but active participants in contests. Recognition of their success in such contests spans centuries and indicates the prestige they enjoyed. Moreover, the extant epigraphical fragments containing lists of contest participants provide vital evidence indicating their influence and fame. These fragments survive primarily as chronicles of victors at literary and oratorical festivals. Evidence from these sources indicates a number of noteworthy facts. Rhapsodes did not fall into disrepute after Plato but continued to thrive as recognized artists. Records from Amphiareion, for example, clearly show that rhapsodes shared honors with tragic and comic actors as well as musicians during the Roman domination of Greece (Enos 1986; Petracos 13, 36–41, 65). Training in the rhapsodic art as a formal study is evident through the third Christian century (*SIG* vol. one, no. 389 [8] duo, no. 424 [10], no. 489 [12], no. 509 [6]; vol. two, no. 711L[32], [no. 736 (42. 150.165]; vol. three, no. 958[36], no. 959 [9]; *OCD* 920). There are even indications at this late date that rhapsodic contests were offered at a wide range of places, varying from contests for children to events held on Chios (*SIG*, vol. three, nos. 958, 959).

Although rhapsodes continued to participate in contests, their function as linguistic guardians of Homeric pronunciation and scholarship diminished. As centuries passed, the Greek language continued to develop, alter, and be influenced by numerous dialects which gradually eroded the oral characteristics of the language from Homeric Greek and made reconstruction increasingly more difficult (Maas 3, 4). Efforts by rhapsodes to maintain the "correct" pronunciation, intonation, accent, and rhythm of Homeric Greek were doomed to failure. From the first century A.D. onward, the quantitative metre which characterized Homeric oral interpretation became further removed from the rhythmical structure of the language. In addition, for some unknown reason, no Greek writer of any importance seems to have concerned himself with metric studies (Maas 3–5).

In a futile attempt to preserve the pronunciation of Homeric Greek, scholars eventually adopted a written system of diacritical notations (stress symbols) to indicate vocal quality and quantity. In spite of these efforts, W. Sidney Allen claims that by "Alexandrian times, as knowledge of the earlier language declined, and as Greek came to be taught as a foreign language, the need was felt for marking such features in classical texts in cases where ambiguity might otherwise result . . . ." (1973, 4). Second century B.C. Alexandrian scholars, such as Zenodotus of Ephesus, and even Byzantine scholars, such as Aristophanes, undertook lexicographical studies to codify and thereby preserve Homeric pronunciation with markings and grammatical explanations (Pfeiffer 174–82; Kindstrand). Written explanations, however, failed to preserve phonetic vocal qualities between vowels—a distinction which is the essence of precise interpretation of the Homeric tongue. Moreover, as quantitative distinctions between vowels continued to become increasingly uncertain, the placing of word accents at regular positions in lines began to occur (Maas 15). Even into the early Christian centuries, rhapsodes persisted in their use of the ancient Homeric tongue, but their pronunciation was far removed from the original Greek vernacular which had been altered by centuries of use and modification. By 400 A.D., "correct" pronunciation was all but nonexistent, and the rhapsodic tradition had deteriorated to such an extent that individuals no longer read according to sounds intuitively familiar to listeners but rather according to artificially contrived stress accents on each written word (Maas 13–15).

Eventually, Homeric metre was dictated by structure not tonal quality. The beneficiaries of the rhapsodic tradition were left with only the form of their language and not the quantitative (syllables based on duration of sound rather than stress) sound which produced it. Efforts of rhapsodes to preserve the oral nature of Homeric Greek, both in practice and also in the theoretical development of notational systems, justifies their association with the history of rhetoric—even if that association reveals nothing more than the historical evolution of thought which preceded the "discovery" of rhetoric so frequently credited to Corax and Tisias.

Chapter **II**

The Evolution of Logography in Hellenic Discourse

The Emergence of Logography

The works of Homer, Hesiod, their fellow aoidoi and the later rhapsodes reveal that rhetoric's characteristics were evident in early Hellenic discourse long before rhetoric was recognized as a discipline. Similar evidence of emerging notions of rhetoric are also apparent in the development of logography (the written composition of speech), particularly with early efforts at historical accounting. When studying the history of rhetoric, students and teachers have traditionally been encouraged to associate logography with the speechwriters of Athens in the fifth and fourth centuries B.C. Yet the rhetoricians and orators of classical Athens, who so influenced the intellectual and social forces of the ancient world that their era is called the golden age of Attic oratory, were actually beneficiaries of a Hellenic literary heritage which was directed toward social persuasion. The genesis of this tradition was the oral poetry of the Homeric bards, whose Hellenic value system is readily identifiable in both the *Iliad* and *Odyssey*. Through the sixth, fifth and fourth centuries B.C., however, *prose* literature (i.e λογογραφία, logography) emerged as a challenging medium of expression for heroic bards and writers. For these next three centuries, Greece developed a tradition of logography which directly affected the intellectual movements of her cultures. The culmination of this

23

evolutionary movement was the emergence and popularization of rhetoric in Attica, best exemplified by one of Athens' most successful and influential instructors, Isocrates. In this chapter, we will explore three topics: a broad look at the evolution of logography, an in depth illustration of Herodotus's account of the Battle of Marathon, and a view of generalized logography as a prelude to systematic rhetoric.

"The first successful essays in popular prose literature," wrote William Mure, "cannot . . . be traced beyond the sixth century B.C." (vol. 4, 51). The first known reference to these essayists occurred in Herodotus's *The Persian Wars* where an early Ionian logographer is called a "fable-writer" or "prose-writer" (2. 134, 143). These early chroniclers, the predecessors and contemporaries of Herodotus himself, seem to have originally derived their name as an indication of their literary distinctiveness from the epic poets. Ionian nomenclature seemed to stress the difference in the literary form of a work (Herodotus 1. 142–43). Prior to this time the *epopoioi*, or those who composed epic poetry, presented an all-encompassing province of literature. The blossoming of such prose writers as the Milesians Cadmus and Dionysius created what J. B. Bury called "logo-poets" or the *logopoioi* who composed in prose (16). As we have seen, Homeric aoidoi and early rhapsodes composed epic poetry orally and only later used writing. *Logographoi*, however, emphasized prose composition and used writing from the beginning as an instrument of composition. The use of writing in prose composition is understandable, since the rhyme of poetry that aids memory in oral composition does not exist to the same degree in prose. The evolution of the term logographoi, then, appears to mean nothing more than to stress the idea that these individuals used some type of writing instrument, which would separate them from their predecessors, the aoidoi and early rhapsodes.

Mythological treatises, geographical and chronological works, local histories and the recording of the behavior and history of non-Greek people were all within the province of the logographers. The emergence of these Ionian pioneers in prose literature is uncertain. The fact that this prose literature did develop and spring forth in Ionia is the only clue to its mysterious birth. Perhaps, as Chester G. Starr argued, early Ionian logographers turned to prose because of its greater suitability to thought than the medium of poetry (106). Whatever the reason, there seems to be an awareness that conversational language did not present the metrical restrictions characteristic of early epic verse (Starr 116; cf. Pearson 6). Yet, "the language of prose," as Strabo wrote, was still "an imitation of the language of poetry," for early prose writers such as Cadmus, Pherecydes, and Hecataeus dropped the meter but retained "all other characteristics of poetry" (Strabo 12. 3, 21; tr. in Pearson 5). The inability of the Ionian prose writers to divorce themselves completely from the characteristics of poetry, their emphasis on myth, legend and popular history prompted Thucydides to remark that these early logographers were not above sacrificing historical accuracy for the sake of euphony (1. 21). This preference for fictive effect over accuracy lead to the sort of storytelling (οἱ λόγοι) that prompted Lionel Pearson to argue that the term "logographer" (ὁ λογογράφος) shifted meaning from a prose-writer to a raconteur, chronicler or historical novelist (Pearson 6).

Not all critics have so stringently criticized the style of these Ionian logographers. Dionysius of Halicarnassus, in his fifth chapter of *De Thucydide*, declared that the object of these eastern, Asian Greeks was "to bring to the general knowledge of the public the written records that they found preserved in temples or in secular buildings in the form in which they found them, neither adding nor taking away anything" (5). Dionysius went on to label this Ionian style as "clear, simple, unaffected . . . and not revealing any elaborate art in composition" (*De Thucydide* 5). Whatever vice ancient or modern critics profess concerning the Ionian logographers, the following observations are important: 1) as Felix Jacoby affirms, ποιηταί (poets) and λογολράφοι (logographers-chroniclers) represented all of sixth century literature (300, n. 28; Thucydides 1. 21. 1, 2); 2) as J. B. Bury argued, the logography in Ionia implied a spaciousness of prose literature that embraced not only history but also such areas as philosophy, science and fables (15); and 3) Ionian logographers never completely divorced themselves from the stylistic ornamentation inherent in the earlier epic poetry. Throughout the sixth, fifth and into the fourth century B.C., the praise or blame which logography — in particular historical composition — received was more a criticism of the logographers' emphasis on style, truth and effect than of their ability to record facts. The reason for this critical perspective is grounded in the close relationship of rhetoric and history.

Ninteenth-century scholar Richard C. Jebb argued that "the relationship between ancient oratory and ancient prose, philosophical, historical or literary, is necessarily of the closest kind . . . [because] prose which was written with a view to being spoken stood in the closest relation with that prose which was written with a view to being read" (Jebb vol. 1, 1xxi). The concept of rhetoric in Greece in the late fifth and early fourth centuries B.C. transcended the modern concept of the art of oratory and should not always be taken in the strict sense of a formal oration delivered in a public assembly. The focus of educational literature, grammar, logic, dialectic and all forms of literary disputations inherent in the Greek concept of *paideia* (intellectual excellence) were subjected to the precepts embodied in rhetorical compositions. Correct composition was a necessity for teaching moral and physical science. Thus, the sophists of the fifth century B.C. were compelled to be rhetors (Mure vol. 4, 98). The close relationship between oral and written communication plus the technological advantages of writing for recording and stabilizing discourse over time made logography as much a medium of rhetorical expression as did public speaking. As civic functions increased—for democracy in cities such as Athens required citizens to argue their cases in court and to actively participate in public assemblies—and as educational sophistication sought to meet those challenges, the role and domain of expression would become much more specialized and discrete. At this nascent period, however, the view of logography was generalized and pervasive.

A century after Thucydides and his contemporaries were educated, Aristotle called rhetoric a derivative art of dialectic utilizing the principles of both ethics and politics (*Rhetoric* 1.2.7). When pupils learned to speak, they also learned to analyze the nature of government and to evaluate old and new ethical standards. Although the principles of rhetoric were expounded in the fourth century B.C., John H. Finley, Jr. maintained that even in the fifth century B.C. subjects such as history did not exist apart from the art of speaking (63). The unifying factor between rhetoric and prose literature, specifically history, was the art of composition, which served as the logical framework for the construction of thought.

Aristotle argues that rhetoric as a system of composition (λέξις) encompassed all prose literature in three basic styles: written composition (λέξις γραφική); the publicly delivered speech, as in forensic oratory ('αγωνιστική); and the panegyric or epideictic form ('επιδεικτική) which dealt with praise or blame (Aristotle, *Rhetoric* 3. 12. 1, 2, 5) and was actually an amalgamation of the first two styles. Aristotle professed that the panegyric style may be spoken, but it is usually "suited to written composition, for its function is reading" (*Rhetoric* 3. 12. 5). The Greeks labeled this style as panegyric or epideictic, wrote Cicero, because compositions of praise, description, history and persuasion were done for display and pleasure, such as the *Panegyricus* of Isocrates (*Orator* 11. 37; cf. Hundson-Williams 251). With rhetoric overshadowing these disciplines it is no wonder, as Hubbell wrote, that history was regarded in antiquity as a branch of rhetoric (333). We have seen that as Greece progressed through the stages of a non-literate, pre-literate to literate culture, rhetoric correspondingly moved from consisting exclusively of oral techniques to incorporating techniques for written composition. Subsumed within this evolution of oral and written communication, history too would be considered one manifestation of rhetoric and take on its own particular features when it evolved to its own form of written discourse.

This early, all-encompassing view of rhetoric colored the concept of logography from the strict reporting of the sixth century B.C. Ionian chroniclers to the polished compositions of such fifth century B.C. historians as Thucydides. Thus, as Bury demonstrated, schools developed which subordinated history, in the Thucydidean sense, to literary "art" (174). Logography had so shifted that "the conventionalists appealed to taste, the realists appealed to the emotions. The former edified, the latter excited. But for both alike history was simply a branch of rhetoric" (Bury 174). In essence, these same aesthetic qualities of epic poetry which so captured Greek listeners for centuries were evident also in historical writing because of its strong ties with rhetoric. Moreover, the misuse of rhetorical precepts of style and embellishment for the sake of artistic achievement could easily evoke a transformation from factual accuracy into an indulgence for ornamentation and affectation that would sacrifice truth for effect. This transformation is evident in the early efforts of historical accounting by Herodotus, the forensic (legal argumentation) logography of Antiphon and in the fourth century B.C. school of Isocrates, which would produce historical novelists and moral storytellers under the guise of historical logographers.

Herodotus, the Father of
Rhetorical Historiography

The scholarship devoted to the historical methods of Herodotus enjoys a long and distinguished history. Much of that work, however, has produced differing opinions about Herodotus's history and his credibility as an historian. Current authorities have sought to resolve these conflicting opinions by introducing a closer analysis that emphasizes not so much the methods employed by Herodotus to chronicle and analyze events but other social, cultural and psychological features. One of the most recent examples of this type of research is Donald Lateiner's *The Historical Method of Herodotus*1989). Lateiner argues that the "creative shaping of the past" (50) by Herodotus constitutes a new genre in Hellenic discourse, one which he sees as nothing less than a new rhetoric (13–51). Lateiner's approach concentrates on narrative style, the use of speeches or *logoi* to illustrate perspectives, and stylistic methods of drawing readers into the text. These technical features reveal an unmistakable awareness of how style affects interpretation; Lateiner's observations provide an excellent illustration of these rhetorical features.

Our emphasis on Herodotus's notions of rhetoric will take a different approach. We will be concerned primarily with the approach of Herodotus toward historical writing rather than specific technical features of his work. Herodotus saw history as argument and used his skills to "account" for monumental events by building a case that uses events as proof of his interpretation. This mentality toward history, moving from the mere chronicling of events to the hermeneutic (interpretative) and jurisprudential (case-building) act of argument reveals an emerging notion of rhetoric that influenced not only his writing but that of future historians as well. In this sense, the unique rhetorical features of Herodotus's history are the consequence of a mentality that viewed historiography differently than the logographers who were his predecessors. This mentality, unique for both its time and task, is most easily understood by examining how his thoughts and sentiments directed his accounts.

The Battle of Marathon, a discrete event within a clearly defined context, provides an excellent example of Herodotus's notion of rhetorical historiography. His bias against the Persian Empire resulted in a pro-Athenian perspective. His intent, evident throughout his account of the battle, was to establish a construct of values that would function as a standard for the diverse views of Hellenic civilization. Herodotus initiated the tradition of a persuasive style of historiography that would have an impact on later educators and historians including Isocrates, Ephoros, and Theopompos. They consciously incorporated principles of rhetoric into their writings for the purpose of fostering panhellenism. In this respect, Herodotus can be considered not only the father of history but also of rhetorical historiography. The perspective of his account reveals the first conscious attempt by a major Greek historian to relate events in a manner designed to direct individuals toward adopting a predetermined attitude. That is, Herodotus illustrates a transition in logography from a generalized chronicling of acts to an interpretative accounting of events, an account which promotes a particular perspective.

Herodotus's "interpretations" of events were not universally accepted. Despite recent recognition of his rhetorical disposition, many scholars considered Herodotus's rhetorical skills negative traits. "Several individuals," wrote Plutarch, "have been thoroughly deceived by the style of Herodotus, . . . but even more people have suffered through his character" since his writing "is the pinnacle of malice" (*De Maligmnitate Herodoti* [*Moralia*] 854). Throughout history, the credibility of Herodotus's account of the Persian wars has been viewed skeptically by critics as eminent as Thucydides (1. 20), Diodorus Siculus (1. 37. 4, 69; 4. 10. 24. 1.), Athenaeus (3. 78E), Aristophanes (*Acharnenses* 513), Plutarch (*De Malignitate Herodoti*), Cicero (*Orator* 39), Quintilian (10. 1. 73), and Dionysius of Halicarnassus (*Epistula ad Pompeium* 3; *De Thucydide* 23); *De Imitatione* 207). Criticism of Herodotus's work has not been limited to ancient scholiasts. Contemporary researchers have also regarded much of his geographical, statistical, and historical accounts as spurious. Yet, scholars have been reluctant to consider rhetoric as a possible explanation for Herodotus's historiography. Much of the contemporary work centers on examining the common technique of Greek historians of presenting "speeches" within the history. Herodotus's rhetorical intent — his effort to present history as a sort of argumentative proof — has been ignored. H. R. Immerwahr, for example, has argued that as an archaic historian, Herodotus would have been unaware of the rhetoric which influenced the later classical period (46). In short, Immerwahr does not recognize that notions of writing persuasive accounts could have existed prior to the establishment of a discipline of persuasion. While Immerwahr did not acknowledge that emerging notions of rhetoric could exist prior to its canonization, other scholars have failed to recognized Herodotus's use of rhetoric by restricting their view of rhetoric. This self-constrained view is best summarized by the Greek historian G. T. Griffith, who argued that "Rhetoric *in the normal sense* [italics mine] of the word as it applied to Greek prose writers, passed him by—thank goodness" (188). If, contrary to the notions of Immerwahr and Griffith, rhetoric can be manifested prior to its disciplinary founding and have meaning other than formulaic techniques employed to attain stylistic eloquence and can be considered more an intentional use of language to persuade, then rhetoric can provide insight of theoretical import in understanding the logography of Herodotus.

Perplexing opinions like those above summarily dismiss a possible explanation for Herodotus's style—that he wrote with a deliberate intent which permeates his entire work. Herodotus wrote his histories decades before the formulaic devices of rhetoric would direct literary and oral expression; yet, the historiography of Herodotus reveals an intent and purpose which is rhetorical in the most generic sense. Herodotus was not attempting to persuade his listeners of the authenticity of his accounts so much as he was trying to synthesize historical events into a perspective which would prescribe and direct a compelling course of action. Herodotus's accounts are lessons which entail guidelines for directing future action. As such, they can be considered rhetorical. An understanding of this viewpoint will not only provide new insights to Herodotus's objectives but will illustrate how nascent notions of rhetoric were employed; his account of the Battle of Marathon is a prime example of such writing.

Herodotus developed and transmitted his historiography from the Ionian alphabetic script which evolved out of an oral tradition. There is clear evidence to support the position that the written script of the Greek phonetic alphabet, which evolved from Phoenician sources, primarily developed in Ionia. In fact, the Ionic alphabet, which Eastern Greek historians including Herodotus used,‛ was officially adopted in Athens during the archonship of Eucleides in 403 B.C. (Fairbank 38–39; Pope 181–83; Ullman 23–31). The strong ties between Ionic and Attic (Athenian) language and culture are important to note, for, as will be discussed later, their bonding helped to foster and disseminate the study of rhetoric through sophists. As a lecturer, Herodotus traveled throughout Greece perpetuating, as Dionysius of Halicarnassus affirms, many of the features of the epic tradition which characterized Homeric literature (De Thucydide 5; Lesky 308; Lucan *Herodotus*; Plutarch *De Malignitate Herodoti* 826). As a beneficiary of the tradition of early Ionian logographers, Herodotus continued the custom of transmitting and preserving his account by recording "tales" or "speeches" [λόγοι] within his writings (Norden 38–41; Solmsen

1943; Solmsen 1944). Such an orally based tradition was understandable, as early Greeks habitually read literary works aloud (Stanford 1, n. 4 ff.; Kennedy 1963, 4; Kirk 1965), 1–32). In effect, Herodotus consciously incorporated oral techniques, which received their genesis from Homeric bards, into his accounts.

Herodotus's techniques or "oral" historiography also convey his worldview and help us to understand his intentions. The implicit intent of Herodotus lies within his perception of the forces which dictate events. One of the dominant forces of causality is human conduct. Herodotus clearly acknowledges the forces of fate (μοῖρα) and chance (τύχη), but (similar to Thucydides) also recognizes the human capacity for choice and the responsibility for consequences (αἴτιος) resulting from individual action (*OCD* 509). The concept of prudent judgment (σωφροσύνη), figures heavily in his analysis (Helen North 27–29; cf. Ranulf vol. 1, 20–33). His portrayal of human causality and the proper code of conduct reveal his rhetorical intent. His objective is to define persuasively the parameters of laudable human action which will function as a construct of societal values.

As a historian, Herodotus was recounting acts which were of firsthand familiarity to many of his contemporaries, and those listeners who fought at Marathon would certainly inhibit an unbridled distortion of events. Herodotus's opening statement attempts to define the province of his work, specifically: "that the great and wondrous accomplishments demonstrated by the Greeks and Barbarians, and particularly that the reason for their confrontation, may not go unnoticed" (1. 1). Unfortunately, the accuracy of Herodotus's information — the objectivity of his reporting — has prompted skepticism over whether he achieved his initial claim (Hammond 1968, 13–57). Herodotus is portrayed as an archaic (pre-classical) historian with the readily apparent Homeric characteristic of praising moral worth on both sides of the battlefield. Ethics, law, and custom were not transitory to Herodotus, and he dutifully acknowledged laudable conduct by Persians.Yet, to assume that overt praise of Persian action indicates a lack of bias would hinder recognition of both his perspective and his rhetoric. Despite the appearance of objectivity, Herodotus's true intent is concealed by his unobtrusive rhetoric.

Herodotus's personal experiences with the Persians provide grounds for his bias against "barbarians." Herodotus was born into a noble family at the Ionian city of Halicarnassus, but strife under the tyrant Lygdamis caused Herodotus to flee the Eastern despotism which oppressed his birthplace (*OCD* 507–9). Lygdamis had ordered the murder of Panyassis, a relative of Herodotus; an action which doubtlessly influenced Herodotus's decision to help expel Lygdamis from his homeland. A recurring theme in Herodotus's account of the Persian wars is the antithetical portrayal of Eastern despotism and Greek freedom (3. 53; 5. 65, 78, 92). For Herodotus, the Persian domination and enslavement of Ionian Greeks violated the right of autonomy and compelled retribution by Greek brethren (1. 169; 3. 80; 4. 142; 5. 92). Herodotus's portrayal of these diametrically opposed cultures clearly establishes the Persians as tyrannical barbarians deserving of retaliatory action, since all Greeks would choose democracy over despotism (4. 137; 5. 92).

Herodotus's bias extended beyond his animosity toward Eastern despotism, the hallmark of the Persian Empire. His Hellenic ties weighed heavily toward Athenian culture. Herodotus considered Athens not only the parent state of all oppressed Ionians but also a model city which had overthrown its own despotic tyrants and replaced them with a system which provided genuine freedom for all citizens (5. 65, 66, 78; 6. 123). He believed that only after Athens established a free political system did she began to manifest her true greatness (6. 113; 5. 65, 66, 78). Herodotus noted the linguistic and cultural similarities shared by the Ionian Greeks and the Athenians. As for Athens' emerging hegemony, he stated that "anyone who says that the Athenians became the saviors of Hellas is not departing from the truth" (7. 139; 1. 142–47). For Herodotus, Persian tyranny threatened to enslave not only all of Ionia and Athens, but all of Greece (6. 109; 7. 138, 157).

The personal misfortune which Herodotus experienced under the shadow of Persian rule was a direct antithesis to the freedom and encouragement he later received from Athens. When Herodotus fled Halicarnassus he settled in the Athenian colony of Thurii in Southern Italy, and soon developed an affinity for the mother city (Aristotle, *Rhetoric* 1409A). As an intellectual center of Greece, Athens attracted the most prominent Hellenic scholars. Lecturing in Athens, Herodotus gained recognition as a prominent educator, developed a friendly relationship with Sophocles, and became one of the city's eminent "honorary citizens" (Plutarch *De Malignitate Herodoti* 826B; Aristophanes *Acharnenses* 513 ff.; Plutarch *Moralia* 785B). His affection toward Athens is evident in his historical accounts (7. 137; 8. 143 ff.; Kleinknecht 241; cf. Lesky 322). These accounts (written primarily in the Ionic dialect) are believed to have been orally presented to Athenian listeners at the Panathenaea in

B.C. 446/445. It is difficult to imagine how Herodotus could be objective when comparing Athenians with Persians, especially since, as John L. Myres argued, "Herodotus neither spoke Persian nor travelled much, if at all, in Persia" (159). (It is possible, however, that Greeks such as Metiochus who were able to communicate with the Persians served as possible sources for Herodotus [6. 41].) Herodotus's personal experiences with Eastern despotism, his intellectual affiliation with Athens, the Athenian audience to whom the work was at least partially directed, and his knowledge of Greek literature (2. 53, 116, 143; 4. 29) all were grounds for an established bias toward Athens.

It was also natural that Herodotus should isolate and give primacy to the Athenians as the representatives of Hellenism. In contrast to the diversity of Greek cities, where mores were modified with every polis, the Persians presented a relatively well-defined social structure. Through his account of Athenian action against Persian despotism, however, Herodotus was able to portray Athens as a model for all Hellas. Thus, the Battle of Marathon, which isolated an almost pure Athenian-Persian confrontation, provided Herodotus with an opportunity to present his assessment persuasively. His observations of these two cultures are presented throughout his work and reveal values that aid in determining the perspective and direction of his rhetorical intent. We can thus trace how he extended logography from the descriptive characteristics of his predecessors to accounts marked by persuasion and argument.

Herodotus drew sharp contrasts between the political sophistication of Athens and that of Persia. When the Athenian runner Phidippides beseeched the Spartans to aid against the oncoming Persian invasion, the herald pleaded "not to permit the most time-honored city in all Greece to be betrayed into slavery by a barbarian culture" (6. 106). "Barbarian" became a constant synonym for the Persian governmental structure. Although the Persian Darius emerged as a king in a society that held vacillating desires toward democracy, oligarchy, and monarchy (3. 82), his autocratic rule could not be favorably regarded by a Greek who was well aware of the oppression of tyrants. A. Andrewes wrote "even a good ruler, like Darius I, who appreciated the quality of the Greeks, could never become their friend as Croesus had been" (116). The Greek Herodotus could see little dignity in a political structure which allowed its king to be chosen by stroking a horse (3. 87) and "held counsel on the most serious matters while intoxicated" (1. 133).

Herodotus's dislike for Persian rule was noticeably contrasted with his high regard for the Athenian political system. His description of Athens's political structure reveals his rhetorical intent. "Athens, which had once been great," wrote Herodotus, "gained even further greatness when the tyrants were deposed" (5. 66). Freedom from autocratic rule was the hallmark by which Herodotus defined the protagonist and antagonist (5. 78). The Persians were despotic, materialistic, and relentless conquerors who crushed Ionian revolts ruthlessly. Athens discarded this type of oppression over her own society and rose up to liberate Greece from the threat of similar subjugation. For Herodotus, this act "clearly demonstrates that when they [the Athenians] were suppressed they allowed themselves to become cowardly, since they served a despot, but once they attained their freedom each one eagerly desired to accomplish as much as he could" (5. 78). It was in the Battle of Marathon that these two political ideologies and cultures clashed in what Herodotus called a question "either to be free or to be enslaved" (6. 11).

Herodotus "Accounts" for the Battle of Marathon

The implications of this Persian-Athenian confrontation became apparent when the Athenian general Miltiades hit upon the political issue of the Battle during his attempt to persuade the *polemarchos* (commanding general) Callimachus to attack the Persian forces: "if they [the Athenians] should submit to the Medes, they will surely suffer, since they will be surrendered to [the tyrant] Hippias, but if they prevail the city will come to be regarded as the foremost city of Greece" (6. 109). Both Persians and Athenians regarded the office of general as military and political (Myres 208). In the Persian military state the generals were appointed and suspended by Darius (6. 43, 119). In Athens, Miltiades could emerge as a general "by the election of citizens" (6. 104). Prior to the battle, the ten tribal Athenian generals (*strategoi*) were divided as to whether to risk a battle with the powerful Persian forces. With the awesome Persian forces only a few miles away, one might expect either an illegal seizure of power by one of the generals or desertions by the tribes. Miltiades, however, took his case to the polemarchos and persuasively won the deciding vote to fight. Even more incredible is that each one of the strategoi—even those "who wished to assume command"—immediately yielded his command privileges to Miltiades following the decision (6. 110); cf. Thucydides 1. 116; Aristotle, *Athenian Constitution* 22).

Herodotus's account reveals that the acts of resolving differences and securing a course of action fostered a persuasive climate. Despite a crisis situation, the course of action was determined by the most credible opinion. In brief, the spirit of free choice was upheld and encouraged even in dire circumstances. For Herodotus, the Athenian mentality assumed that expediency should not determine submission to authority. This atmosphere for open discourse was not limited to the crisis at Marathon. A parallel situation is presented in Herodotus's account of the Battle of Salamis (8. 40–99) as well as complementary accounts by Plutarch (*Vitae Parallelae: Themistocles; Vitae Parallelae: Aristides*). Even with the supreme command, Miltiades would not attack until the day of his generalship arrived—such a situation would be unheard of within the Persian ranks. Herodotus's point is clear: Darius's argument for the supreme command of one man rested on what he considered to be the inherent value of expediency in an autocratic state (3. 82). Yet, Herodotus demonstrated that free men, even in a battle situation, could still exercise the unity required but within the construct of a society devoid of tyranny.

The Persians and Athenians differed not only in political sophistication but also in culture. Possessing no images of their gods, temples, or even altars, the Persians dismissed the human characterization of Athenian gods as pure folly (1. 131). Through a herald named Tomyris, the Persians are further portrayed as expansionistic and militaristic, a people who "will do anything rather than be at peace" (1. 206). In essence, Herodotus portrayed Persian culture as an imperialistic and militarily-oriented society which was subject to the dictates of an absolute ruler who encouraged an attitude of arrogant superiority over other cultures.

Conversely, Herodotus's account portrayed an Athenian culture which markedly emphasized a different set of social norms acceptable to his Hellenic listeners. Herodotus contrasted the Athenians and Persians in the first book when the Athenian lawgiver Solon met the Lydian King Croesus. Solon's explanation to Croesus enabled Herodotus to present a construct of the Athenian value system. In the words of Solon, Tellus was the happiest man because:

Tellus's city was well off and his children were beautiful and
virtuous, and he saw all these children give birth and become
fully established; but this man, having as prosperous a life as
any of us, culminated his life in a most magnificent manner,
for during a battle between the Athenians and the neighboring
Eleusinians, he hastened into battle and put the enemy to flight;
after which, he died most honorably and the Athenians gave him
a public burial and greatly honored him at the very site where
he fell (1. 30).

Generations later, Aristotle would praise Solon in the
Nichomachean Ethics for his superior analysis of these intellectual
and moral virtues which constitute "happiness" (1100A, 1102A,
1102B). A superiority which, for Herodotus, escaped the Persian
mentality. Through this speech by Solon, and Herodotus's praise
of the Athenian lawgiver, we are offered an insight into the values
praised by the author and the motivation for their "democratic"
fight in the Battle of Marathon. Admittedly, other value systems,
such as the Persian, were described throughout his work, but these
alien cultural systems were presented by Herodotus as curious
behavior. If an alien value such as bravery was openly accepted in
Athens, then Herodotus would praise the attribute.

Analyzing Herodotus's account of the Athenian role in the Battle
of Marathon illustrates the author's perspective. First, even though
Sparta was unable to give support because of a religious festival
and Aegina had submitted to the Persian forces, Athens became
"directly motivated" (6. 49). It was Athens which temporarily
assumed the role of protector and, according to Andrew Robert
Burn, literally rushed twenty-six miles to answer the battle cry
(242). Second, although Herodotus gave no figures regarding the
size of the two armies, he did imply that the Athenians were
decidedly outnumbered (6. 109). The disproportionate odds,
compounded by a succession of Persian victories due to their alleged
military superiority, provided a suitable arena for the Athenians to
practice their values. It is no wonder that Herodotus wrote that
"prior to this, the Greeks shuddered at even hearing the name
'Medes'" (6. 112).

The complete victory of the Athenians at Marathon fulfilled
Solon's expressed ideal values. As in Solon's earlier description of
Tellus, the Athenians at Marathon came to the assistance of their
city when it was threatened and succeeded in routing the enemy.
The Athenians were quick to label those who surrendered to the
Persians, as in the case of the Aeginetans, as traitors to Greece

(6. 49). Like Tellus, "many other famous Athenians" (6. 114), gloriously perished in battle and were highly honored; in this case the honor came from the late-arriving Lacedaemonians (6. 120; Vanderpool 1966 and 1966). To their own credit, the same battle-weary Athenians marched from Marathon to the defense of their city immediately after the fight. Herodotus's description of these Athenian soldiers exemplified many of Solon's qualifications that lead to "happiness." In contrast, the barbarians, routed and killed in flight by the disciplined Athenian forces, presented little for Herodotus to praise.

The final contrasting Athenian-Persian value was the solidarity of purpose through unification. In this respect, the Athenians not only surpassed the Persians, but all other Greeks as well. Prior to the Athenian-Persian confrontation at Marathon every other Greek *polis* had failed to defeat the Persians. The underlying cause in each one of these unsuccessful attempts was the failure of the states to unite. This lack of unity was emphasized by Herodotus. The author considered Thracians, excluding the Indians, the largest group of people in the world, "and if they were ruled under one individual or possessed a solidarity [of purpose] against their opponents, I believe that they would be invincible and would be considered the mightiest nation of all" (5. 3). Yet, because these Thracians could not unite, they became easy prey for the Persian commander Megabazus. Like the Thracians, the Ionians failed to break the bonds of Persian control primarily because they lacked unity. The Samians were also incapable of ordering their forces and, at the Battle of Lade, deserted in the face of the Persian fleet. Although submission to Persian forces was detested, Herodotus demonstrated that Greeks such as the Aeginetans lacked solidarity of purpose and were forced to give "earth and water to Darius" in submission (6. 49). Even mighty Sparta suffered under a dual kingship (6. 52). The result was that Sparta's powerful army was often nullified and misdirected by strife: exemplified by the divided kingship of Cleomenes and Demaratus (6. 61).

Herodotus presented the Athenian forces as the unifying power against Persian despotism, although Athens was not absolved from internal disunity. The strife between the Alkmeonidai and Philaidae severely arrested the direction of the city during the crisis. Andrew Robert Burn wrote, "Everyone knew that there were divisions in Athens. The Alkmeonidai, jealous of Miltiades, were in touch with Hipparchos" (239). Yet, although the political strife at home may not have been completely resolved, it was to the credit of the

Athenians that they alone were the first Greek state to present a substantially united force against the Persian army. The ability of the Athenian generals to cast aside their divided opinions and willingly unite against the Persians epitomized the Athenian solidarity of purpose which was instrumental in their victory. In the speech convincing the polemarchos Callimachus to cast his deciding vote to fight, Miltiades eloquently pleaded for the unified commitment which would bring victory: "if we engage them [the Persians] before any corruption can emerge in some Athenians, let the gods deal with us fairly and we will prevail in this encounter" (6. 109).

The solidarity of purpose seen in the Athenian forces was contrasted with Herodotus's portrayal of the Persian army. If the Persian army could be called united, the construct of their unity was established upon different premises than those of the Athenian forces. Where the Athenians had a vested interest in defending their homeland, the Persians and Ionians were compelled to fight because of the imperialistic design of their absolute ruler. Contrasted with the Persian allies, the Plataeans freely chose to ally with the Athenians at Marathon (6. 108). Those Greeks who allied with the Persians, however, were often forced to fight against their brethren because of their submission to Persian tyranny (6. 49). Herodotus explained that all Greeks were united by the common brotherhood of language, religion, and character (8. 144), but it was the solidarity of purpose exhibited by the Athenians that allowed them to gain the first major reversal in the war. In brief, Herodotus portrayed — or perhaps revealed — an Athenian spirit of unity which manifested itself in a virtuous and united defense of freedom and ultimately emerged as one of the prime forces in their victory at Marathon.

Throughout Herodotus's works the Greek world witnessed the emergence of a unified Athenian power which checked the Persian threat and eventually led the Greek states to complete victory. At the conclusion of the work, the Spartans, regarded as the guardians of the Hellenic world, were anxious to return home and set sail for Greece. The Athenians, however, doggedly pursued the enemy until the Persians were completely vanquished (9. 114). Out of Herodotus's account, the Battle of Marathon became not only the pivotal point of the war but also an arena in which Athens could dramatize the most positive aspects and fundamental qualities for a coherent Greek value system. Herodotus's contrast between both the polis against the awesome Persian Empire and freedom against tyranny lauded Athens as the emerging force of Greek unity.

Herodotus's intent, evident throughout his account of the Battle of Marathon, was to establish a construct of values unobtrusively that would function as a standard for the diverse world views of Hellenic civilization. In this respect, Herodotus portrayed Athenian valor in such a manner that Athenian actions at Marathon could be perceived by Greek listeners as a personification of the panhellenic standard of excellence. In brief, Herodotus initiated a tradition of a persuasive style of historiography that would have an impact on such historians as Isocrates, Ephoros, and Theopompos. As we shall see, they consciously incorporated principles of rhetoric into their writings for the purpose of fostering panhellenism. In view of these events, Herodotus can be considered not only the father of history, but also the father of rhetorical historiography. The perspective of his account reveals the first conscious attempt by a major Greek historian to relate events in such a manner that they direct individuals toward adopting a predetermined attitude.

Logography as a Prelude to Systematic Rhetoric

The songs of Homer and the odes of the rhapsodes were all directed toward praise of virtue over vice. The use of what would later be formally termed rhetoric as a means of directing listeners/readers to a particular point of view also provides a demonstration of early efforts toward a techne of rhetoric. The movement from poetic composition to prose evident in the works of logographers — while directed toward more immediate and pragmatic concerns — also displayed systematic techniques that would direct the thoughts and sentiments of listeners. With Herodotus we see a similar strain: the effort to construct prose that moves from a chronicling of events to a directed and interpreted accounting which inherently posits an explanation and judgment of why such happenings occurred. The manipulation and composition of discourse was directed to such ends and Herodotus's nascent efforts in what we call history exemplify early rhetorical efforts. By the very next generation, Thucydides' *Peloponnesian War* revealed a refinement in the art of historiography to a degree that surpassed Herodotus, in terms of accuracy, insight and use of rhetoric. However, Herodotus's early efforts show the development of such traits — the beginning of a rhetorical vector stimulated by the evolution of oral and written composition discussed earlier. This endemic relationship of historiography and rhetoric is evident not only in composition prior to Aristotle but also in schools of thought which would overtly recognize the emerging art of history as a rhetorical activity.

It is not so much that as prose literature and oratory developed into disciplines that they then became rhetorical, for rhetorical traits are evident in the poetry of Homer and the prose of Herodotus's history. It is clear, however, that the sophistication and systematic use of rhetoric—particularly for purposes of interpretation and judgment—are much more consciously directed in subsequent efforts. Later writers and orators reveal in their increased specialization and consciousness attention to human, as opposed to divine, creation of discourse. Sensitive to both his audience and community, Herodotus posited the first clear coexistence of rhetoric with democracy. His accounting of the Battle of Marathon extends the attention to the importance of rhetoric from individual human capacity to the benefits of rhetorical deliberation for a city and her culture. The relationship of rhetoric and society would, in fact, be the central force in the formalization of rhetoric into a discipline, as the next chapter reveals.

Chapter *III*

The Birth of Hellenic Rhetoric and the Growth of the Sicilian Sophistic

Sicily and the Formation of Rhetoric as a Discipline

> There is a firm ancient tradition, still repeated in Roman times by Cicero and Quintilian, that the many lawsuits which ensued [in Syracuse] led to the development of forensic oratory and the first rhetorical handbooks. Whether the cause-and-effect explanation is correct or not, it is a fact that Corax of Syracuse and his pupil Tisias were the founders of the Greek art of rhetoric at this time and that later in the century Gorgias of Leontini was its most famous exponent in the Greek world
> (M. I. Finley, *A History of Sicily: Ancient Sicily*, 61).

There is a good argument to be made that much of the history of Europe is centered in Sicily. From the earliest colonization by the Phoenician "Sea People" that evolved into the Carthagenian civilization, from colonization by Greeks and later the Romans, as the seat of the Holy Roman Empire to its strategic importance in World War II, Sicily has somehow been involved in every major force in European history. Sicily has played the role of victim, patron and beneficiary while buffeted by these forces. It also played a key

41

role in the history of rhetoric in the West. Rhetoric was formalized into a discipline in Sicily and from there its influence spread throughout the Hellenic world and eventually through Western history itself.

Sicily was the center for a confluence of various modes of expression—all of which demonstrated some traits of rhetorical techniques if not yet a formalized techne. The poetry of Homer and later aoidoi and rhapsodes, the increasing sophistication of logographers and the emergence of a bona fide historiography with Herodotus illuminate a path to a system of structuring discourse. The increasing interest in democracy heightened sensitivity to the ability for oral expression as a source of power in the operations of civic and judicial functions. Sicily's encouragement of artistic patronage, the diverse forms of government operating in her cities, and her attractiveness for conquest and colonization by mainland Greek cities created an atmosphere and opportunity to systematize and develop rhetoric as a discipline. It will become apparent, however, that such developments came about for a variety of intellectual, political, and social reasons.

Unlike almost every other study of phenomena that involve Sicily, the accounts of rhetoric's origins there are inadequately represented in the tumultuous history that shaped the island's destiny. M. I. Finley's otherwise excellent volume, *Ancient Sicily*, offers only one page about rhetoric, Corax, Tisias and Gorgias. Finley is too fine an historian and rhetoric is too important to the shaping of Sicily's history—and for that matter the history of Greece itself—to be limited to such an incomplete treatment. Understanding rhetoric's emergence as a discipline in Sicily and the impact of the Sicilian Sophistic on the spread of rhetoric throughout the Hellenic world can only result from a knowledge of the political and social context at the time. Perhaps more distressing than the minimal treatment by many historians are works by current rhetoricians that attempt an historical perspective by relying on anecdotal accounts which do little justice either to the political and social forces operating in ancient Sicily or to the historical evidence that would help replace folklore with accurate accountings.

Rhetoric's origin as a formal discipline is best understood as an evolution of compositional techniques. Social and political forces provided both the environment and exigence for the development of pragmatic techniques which eventually coalesced into a discipline. The interaction of these forces help to explain both rhetoric's origins and the formation of the Sicilian Sophistic itself.

Despite its sustained influence in shaping Western thought, the history of rhetoric as a discipline has relied primarily on anecdotal stories and persistent legends—much of which come from and depend upon extant literary sources. Primarily through efforts brought about by historical research and archaeological excavations done during this century, new sources on Greece's past are available. Frequently these epigraphical sources—inscriptions composed on such durable material as marble—have been unearthed along with other physical remains at archaeological sites. Unlike literary texts transmitted and altered by generations of scribes and scholars, these physical artifacts (while sometimes recorded) often remain on site and unaltered from their original composition. As such, they constitute new and direct evidence about rhetoric in ancient Greece.

Other obstacles have made it difficult to study the emergence of rhetoric in Sicily. The development of oral literature in ancient Greece predates accurate historical accounts, requiring scholars to limit their observations to little more than inferences and speculation about the techniques and development of composition. The evolution to rhetoric, as we have seen, came about over centuries and through different forms of expression. Yet the discipline of rhetoric—the formalized art which advances systematic techniques for oral and written discourse—has a traditionally accepted point of origin that is identified in time and place as occurring near the first quarter of fifth century B.C. in Greece. Two locations, Sicily and Athens, figure prominently in the formation of rhetoric. In Sicily, the cities of Syracuse and Leontini played major roles: Corax and Tisias were from Syracuse; Gorgias was from Leontini. Athens, the intellectual and cultural center of the Hellenic world, did much to promote and popularize rhetoric— both in her relationship with Sicilian cites and throughout the Greek-speaking world. Unfortunately, this specificity is based on the perpetuation of traditional legends and not accurate historiography. As such, and despite rhetoric's widespread acceptance, little evidence has been gathered and systematically studied to determine rhetoric's origins. Tacit acceptance of stories have not only made for an incomplete explanation of rhetoric's beginning but have failed to account adequately for the cultural and political forces that interacted with and influenced the emergence of literacy and the consciousness of discourse. Rhetoric's birth is best understood not as an isolated event but rather as a continuum of emerging consciousness about discourse dating from *Homerica,* through the Pre-Socratics and into the Classical Period of Greece, which marked the first instance of public literacy. The formalization of rhetoric into a discipline in Sicily and subsequently Athens, then, marks a point in the development of the awareness of the importance of discourse in social interaction and intellectual growth.

Two major bodies of research on this topic exist for tracing the origins of rhetoric: scholarship on the history of ancient Sicily and research on the early history of Hellenic rhetoric. Unfortunately, these two bodies of scholarship have remained, for all practical purposes, autonomous. As a result, historical accounts do not acknowledge rhetoric as a social force. Likewise, discussions of rhetoric's history do not adequately recognize the cultural forces that shaped its development.

The oldest (and still among the best) historical treatment is Edward A. Freeman's four volume work, *The History of Sicily* (1891–1894). Recent archaeological and historical scholarship have added to Freeman's contributions. T. J. Dunbabin, a half-century after Freeman's seminal scholarship, provided a revised history based largely on archaeological findings in *The Western Greeks* (1948). More recent work, continuing to synthesize and integrate new evidence, is offered in A. G. Woodhead's *The Greeks in the West* (1962), John Boardman's *The Greeks Overseas* (1964), and Moses I. Finley's readable but general *A History of Sicily: Ancient Sicily* (1968). Margaret Guido's *Sicily: An Archaeological Guide* (1967) provides an excellent (but now dated) summary of archaeological research. Current scholarship offers more specialized study, such as Brian Caven's *Dionysius I: War-Lord of Sicily* (1990). Here, as in the other scholarship mentioned above, the nature and impact of rhetoric is virtually ignored. Caven mentions rhetoric only twice (16, 20) when offering off-hand comments about Corax and Gorgias. The works mentioned above take somewhat different approaches ranging from informative, general accounts to specific research. While each makes substantial contributions to our historical knowledge of Sicily and her place in the Hellenic world, this century-long scholarship virtually ignores the role of rhetoric in Sicily's history and her contributions through Sicilian sophists to the Hellenic world.

Just as historians of Sicily have ignored rhetoric, historians of rhetoric such as Kennedy (1963, 1980, 1991), Vickers (1988), and Conley (1990) show no apparent familiarity with the research mentioned above. They have neither advanced rhetoric's history by the assimilation of historical, archaeological and epigraphical scholarship nor offered recent primary work of their own on this topic. This shortcoming is evident even in the most recent contribution of Thomas Cole, *The Origins of Rhetoric in Ancient Greece* (1991). His interpretations like those mentioned above are limited to the standard accounts of rhetoric's history and are restricted to conventional literary sources. While the scholarship is competent, the sources of study, particularly historical and archaeological work, are limited.

These limitations have produced a gap in our knowledge about rhetoric. Incorporating the missing historical and cultural evidence would provide a more thorough account of rhetoric's origins and growth than is possible from the re-evaluation of standard literary sources. In her recent book, *Rereading the Sophists: Classical Rhetoric Refigured*, Susan C. Jarratt clearly emphasizes how the sophists have been "eclipsed in histories of rhetoric" (xviii), calling for a greater sensitivity to the sophists' political role in the "foundation of democracy" (9) and the need for historians to expand their "range of materials" in order to make more sensitive observations (13).

Forces that Shaped Sicily's Rhetorical Climate

The forces shaping the emergence of rhetoric in Sicily, its popularization among Sicilian cities—particularly Syracuse and Leontini—and its eventual transmission to Athens and mainland Greece was generated not so much by lively intellectual motives as by political manipulation. Rhetoric was recognized as a source of political power in two respects: first, as an instrument for overthrowing monarchial and tyrannical governments and replacing them with democracies; and second, as a source of power within democracies, where control of public opinion through proficiency in discourse was essential. The wealth and strategic importance of Sicily made her attractive to several Greek city-states. Athens in particular recognized the benefits of supporting and nurturing democracies. Incompatible political forces inevitably prompt conflict. Syracuse and Leontini with their colliding histories are excellent examples of opposing forces which shaped not only the history of Sicily but the growth of rhetoric itself.

In many respects, Syracuse and Leontini are a study in contrast. Syracuse, with a long history of affiliation with Corinth, was a commercial and cultural force. Her eventual defeat of Athens influenced the course of Greek history itself. Aside from brief episodes of democracy, Syracuse was governed by tyrants, whose rule and success were in direct opposition to the principles and interests of Athenian democracy. Leontini, by contrast, had a long-established affiliation with Athens. When contrasted with Syracuse, it was a relatively minor city in the shaping of both Sicily's history and Western civilization—except in the history of rhetoric. The interaction of these two cities illuminate the climate from which rhetoric emerged, the reasons for its formalization, and the role that Athens played in its dissemination.

Our record of the Greek colonization of Sicily is based primarily on the work of Thucydides. In Book VI of *The Peloponnesian War*, he provided a chronology of Hellenic settlement on the island. Thucydides tells us (6.3) that Naxos was the first Greek settlement on the island of Sicily, followed by Syracuse and Leontini. Naxos and Leontini were founded by the Chalcidians under Theokles, and Syracuse was founded by the Corinthians. Both Naxos and Syracuse offered excellent ports; the commercial advantages were obvious. Leontini, as Dunbabin notes (46), is the only original Greek colony to be settled inland, near the river Symaithos but approximately six miles from the sea.

Leontini's tremendous advantage and attraction was its strategic location in the rich Laistrygonian plain. Sicily has been called "the birth-place of wheat," so abundant that it was said to have grown wild (Dunbabin 212). The *campi Leontini* was the most fertile area in Sicily (Diodorus Siculus 5. 2), so prosperous that Leontini's wealth was literally proverbial: "ἀεὶ Λεοντῖνοι περὶ τοὺς κρατῆρας" (Diogenianus, *Paroemiae* 2. 50; Dunbabin 319, n. 2)). Leontini's rich, wheat-producing area would be of considerable interest to commercially-oriented Greek cities. In fact, there is some evidence that Leontini had been exporting wheat to Greece before any colonization (Dunbabin 10). Athens' long-standing interest and support of Leontini was undoubtedly motivated by her strategic position, commercial resources, and interest in democracy. It is easy to understand why, as Thucydides observed, Athens was always friendly to Leontini (6. 46, 76) and stood ready to serve as an ally to Leontini against Syracuse as an excuse for pursuing her expansionist interests on the island.

It is also important to note the cultural differences in the early original settlements. Naxos and Leontini (originally occupied by the native Sicels) were founded by Chalcis, a principal city on the island of Euboea and an important commercial center. Because of its

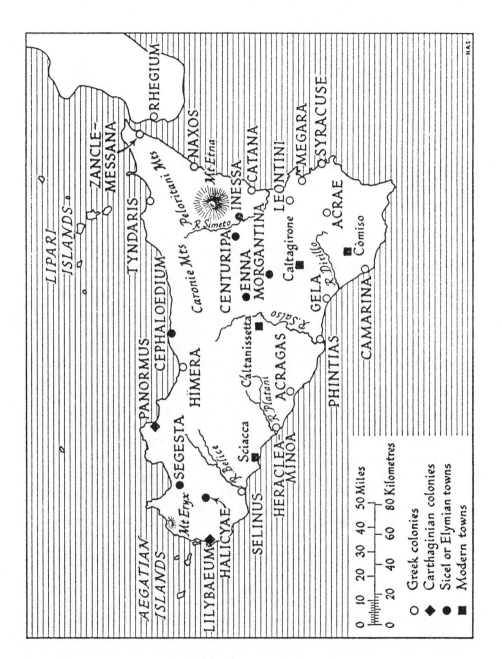

proximity to Athens, Euboea was viewed as sharing strong ancestral ties with Ionia. In fact, their common Ionic bonding served as motivation for Athenian support of Leontini (Thucydides 3. 86). As we shall see later, the embassy headed by Gorgias to Athens in 427 B.C. was based on that established relationship and Gorgias's sophisticated use of rhetoric was enhanced by his dialect fluency (Enos 1990). The importance of this dialect bonding cannot be overemphasized, for that Attic-Ionic tie was not only an advantage in Gorgias's popularity in Athens but also an inducement to spread the principles of rhetoric emerging out of the Sicilian sophistic through the Attic-Ionic dialect and throughout the Greek world (Enos 1990). Conversely, Syracuse's Doric origins would be in opposition to the identification fostered by the Ionic heritage shared between Leontini and Athens.

Political factors intensified social and cultural differences and provided situations within which rhetoric could emerge as a source of power. Naxos and Syracuse were, as mentioned, both founded at about 734 B.C. (Thucydides 6. 3; c. f. Miller 276–277) and the two cities maintained their ties throughout the classical period. The early government of Syracuse was controlled by a privileged class called *gamoroi*. Although these aristocrats held power into the fifth century B.C., they were eventually (albeit briefly) overthrown by a democratic revolution. Gelon, one of the strong supporters of this democratic revolt, became a tyrant of immense popularity (Diodorus Siculus 11. 67. 2–5) who succeeded in strengthening Syracuse and building a powerful navy. Gelon's brother, Hieron I, building on the strength of Gelon's rule, became a patron of the arts and helped to make Syracuse a city of patrons who attracted several poets, orators and artists such as Aeschylus, Simonides, Pindar and (eventually) even Plato. Pindar's *Olympian Odes* 1 and *Pythian Odes* 2 and 3 were composed under the patronage of Hieron to celebrate his victories in the horse and chariot races of the Olympic and Pythian Games. Pindar's poetic encomia provide an indirect but vivid illustration of artistic patronage in Syracuse under Hieron's tyranny (Gold 22–27).

Sicily was very attractive to those facile in eloquent expression. The early patronage for which Sicily became famous throughout the Hellenic world, particularly as popularized through such national festivals as the Olympic and Pythian Games, both nurtured and underscored her reputation. This long-standing patronage in the arts of rhetoric and poetry inspired gifted Sicilians to go forth from their native island and seek patronage throughout Greece.

Under these social and economic conditions, we can see that Sicily provided the ideal environment to nurture and support sophists who would benefit from the island's reputation in both attracting and producing the most gifted artists of eloquent expression. In this respect, the environment that produced Gorgias was enhanced through a heritage of patronage. As mentioned earlier, that same environment served as the basis for effective political and legal expression when democratic political interest overcame the tyrants of various Sicilian cities. When democracies were repressed by new tyrannies or oligarchies, individuals effective in legal and political rhetoric could convert their oral and literate skills to more artistic and administrative functions.

Although Hieron's rule of Syracuse did not provide the environment for free expression of democratic practice, it did value eloquence and attracted skilled orators. The immense popularity of rhetoric had a clear practical utility under the democratic conditions that followed Hieron's brother, the "violent and murderous" Thrasybulus (Diodorus Siculus 11. 67. 5). He became tyrant in 467/66 B.C. but was quickly deposed and a democracy was established that would thrive, by varying accounts, from forty to sixty years. It is precisely at this time—when tyranny was replaced by democracy—that rhetoric was "invented" in Syracuse. The patronage of rhetoric as an art form popularized during the reigns of Gelon and especially Hieron was transformed into a practical craft necessary for the workings of a successful democracy. The dissolutions of the great kingdoms in Greek Sicily and the general recall of exiles necessitated, as Caven notes (14), the reappointment of land (*ges anadasmos*). The litigation and policy making necessary to resolve disputes was the perfect environment to foster effective training in rhetoric. Democracy in Syracuse—as it was throughout much of the ancient world—was a fragile condition. While resistance to tyranny persisted, so did Syracuse's strong oligarchic sentiment. Riddled with demagogues and informers, the delicate balance of distributed power necessary for democracy was too tenuous to sustain. The upper class had ample opportunity to regain power. The eventual result was a return to tyranny (Caven 16) under the tremendously successful Dionysius.

Although Leontini's foundation as a city was similar to that of Syracuse, its political growth and history were different, although intertwined. As noted earlier, the Chalcidians first established Naxos and then founded Leontini. The Chalcidians were known for their alphabet (Boardman 201) and doubtlessly would have nurtured a literate culture. Both Naxos and Leontini established close and enduring ties with Athens, providing that city with allies as a base for Athenian expansion into commercially rich and fertile Sicily. Diodorus Siculus (12. 54. 1-7) was convinced that this motivation directed Athenian support and activity. Diordorus' view has some support from Thucydides (3. 86), who believed that Leontini's rich agricultural benefits — particularly grain — were attractive to Athens (Finley 66–67; Boardman 183–184). Long threatened and dominated by Corinthian-supported Syracuse, Leontini regained independence in 464 B.C., fortified herself against Syracuse, and entered an alliance with Athens.

The long-standing Athenian political interest in Sicily was critical to the introduction of rhetoric at Athens and its subsequent spread throughout the Hellenic world. Athenians had held a strong interest in Sicily as far back as the mid-fifth century B.C. (Finley 66), signing treatises with such cities as Segesta, Halicyae, Rhegium (across in mainland Italy) and Leontini. Athens reaffirmed her treaties with cities such as Rhegium and Leontini in 433/32 B.C., but it was clear that Sicilian cities were aligning either with Corinthian-supported Syracuse or Athenian-supported Leontini and that a conflict was imminent. War broke out between Syracuse and Leontini in 427 B.C. — the year that Gorgias headed his famous embassy to Athens. Athens demonstrated her support by sending twenty ships to Sicily under Laches and Charoeades (Thucydides 3. 86). Other Sicilian cites drew up alliances with either Syracuse or Leontini. Himera, Gela, Locri and (perhaps) Selinus sided with Syracuse while Kamarina, Catania, Naxos and Rhegium (Southern Italy) sided with Leontini (Finley 66–67). Athens reinforced her commitment to democratic Leontini in 425 B.C. with forty-five ships. A year later, the Sicilian cities — likely fearing the ever-increasing external entanglements with mainland Greek cities — convened a peace conference at Gela and temporarily resolved differences. A civil war in Leontini in 422 B.C. provided the wealthier classes in Leontini with an opportunity to solicit Syracuse's support in crushing the democracy and establishing an oligarchy under Syracuse's control. Examining the parallel political events of Syracuse and Leontini reveals relationships between political forces which created the opportunity for supporters of democracy to understand the pragmatic aspects of rhetoric.

It is obvious that these series of events are critical to both Sicily's history and rhetoric's as well. Peace delegations were employed to try to resolve political differences among Sicilian cities. When war

Syracuse
485–478 B.C.
The tyrant Gelon establishes Syracuse as a strong city with a powerful navy.

478–467 B.C.
Gelon's brother, Hieron I, succeeds as tyrant and the arts flouris.

467/466 B.C.
Hieron's brother, the "violent and murderous" Thrasybulus, becomes tyrant but is quickly deposed.

467/466 B.C.
Rhetoric "invented" by Corax and Tisias in Syracuse.

466–415 B.C.
Syracuse and other Sicilian cities ruled under tyrants governing with democratic procedures (possible Athenian influence and support).

427 B.C.
Embassy sent to Athens from Syracuse (Tisias) and Leontini (Gorgias).

415 B.C.
War with Athens, Syracuse is victorious.

Leontini
Early 5th Century B.C.
Leontini, rich and prosperous, is attacked by Hippocrates of Gela, and is eventually dominated by Syracuse.

464 B.C.
Leontini regains independence, fortifies against Syracuse, and enters an alliance with Athens (democratic principles guide the government).

433/32 B.C.
Leontini formalizes democratic alliance with Athens through treaty agreements.

427–424 B.C.
Syracuse besieges Leontini, embassy to Athens from Syracuse (Tisias) and Leontini (Gorgias).

422 B.C.
Internal strife results in a dependency on Syracuse.

415–413 B.C.
Syracuse's victory over Athens dashes Leontini's hope for independence.

came, Sicilians again sought to settle disputes through peace conferences. If such accounts are accurate, we see the esteem for rhetoric in Sicily. Most accounts credit the resolution of land disputes as the reason for rhetoric's emergence as a formal discipline in Syracuse in 467 B.C., but the peace delegations and conferences demonstrate that rhetoric was recognized as a deliberative source of power as well. Thus, rhetoric's rationale for existence and popularization was heightened by both its forensic and deliberative power. The eventual emergence of Sicilian sophists would transform its political power and demonstrate its instructive and epideictic strength as practiced in education and performed in social celebrations and contests (Enos 1986).

Rhetoric as an Enabling Tool for Political Power

At this point, we have strong reasons to believe that accounts confirming the legend of Gorgias of Leontini travelling to Athens in 427 B.C. are accurate. We have examined the political forces that prompted his trip. It is clear that at a time when democracy did not flourish in cities such as Syracuse, rhetoric and the language arts in general were supported for artistic reasons. Rhetoric was gradually transformed from a patron-supported art to a political tool of power used in the creation and operation of democracy. When Gorgias represented Leontini at Athens, he did so as a sanctioned official of a democratic city and used his oratorical skills to sustain Athenian support based upon an earlier treaty. After fulfilling his political duties, Gorgias utilized that same power in rhetoric to shape an educational force that would flourish as naturally in the democracy of Athens as it had in Leontini. In his dialogue *Gorgias*, Plato challenged Gorgias's power of rhetoric not only on intellectual grounds but also as a political source of power. Plato did not want rhetoric to operate as a paideia—a standard of intellectual excellence—in Athens. Plato recognized that the intellectual issues upon which he challenged rhetoric's credibility were intertwined with its political power and could be as easily converted to political control of democratic mob rule as it had been in Sicily. Thus, when Plato went to Syracuse to train Dionysius's son to be a philosopher-king, he had no intention of supporting either a democracy or rhetoric. His fears were embodied in Gorgias of Leontini whose powerful rhetoric created lasting political and intellectual effects.

The explanation of rhetoric's emergence and popularity presented above is grounded in pragmatic, self-serving political motives with an emphasis on the political/democratic ties between Athens and Leontini. While the consistency of historical accounts offered above provide strong support for this view, recently discovered epigraphical evidence offers additional and irrefutable testimony of the accuracy of this interpretation. The (officially authorized) photograph of the Athenian-Leontini treaty published and reproduced on the cover by permission of the Ministry of Culture of the Greek Government, verifies the alliance, renewed under the archonship of Aphseudos in 433/32 B.C.

[ΘΕ]ΟΙΠΡΕΣΒΕΣ ΕΓΛΕΟΝ[Τ]—
ΙΝΟΝΗΟ[Ι]ΤΕΓΧΣΥΜΜΑΧΙ
ΑΝΕΠΟΕΣΑΝΤΟΚΑΙΤΟΝΗ
ΟΡΚΟΝΤΙΜΕΝΟΡΑΓΑΘΟΚ
ΛΕΟΣΣΟΣΙΣΓΛΑΥΚΙΟΓΕ
ΛΟΝΕΧΣΕΚΕΣΤΟΓΡΑΜΜΑ
ΤΕΥΣΘΕΟΤΙΜΟΣΤΑΥΠΙΣ
ΚΟΕΠΑΦΣΕΥΔΟΣΑΡΧΟΝΤ
ΟΣΚΑΙΤΕΣΒΟΛΕΣΗΕΙΚΡ
ΙΤΙΑΔΕΣΕΓΡΑΜΜΑΤΕΥΕ
ΕΔΟΧΣΕΝΤΕΙΒΟΛΕΙΚΑΙ
ΤΟΙΔΕΜΟΙΑΚΑΜΑΝΤΙΣΕ
ΠΡΥΤΑΝΕΥΕΧΑΡΙΑΣΕΓΡ
ΑΜΜΑΤΕΥΕΤΙΜΟΧΣΕΝΟΣ
ΕΠΕΣΤΑΤΕΚΑΛΛΙΑΣΕ
ΙΠΕΤΕΜΜΕΝΧΣΥΜΜΑΧΙΑ
ΝΕΙΝΑΙΑΘΕΝΑΙΟΙΣΚΑΙ
ΛΕΟΝΤΙΝΟΙΣΚΑΙΤΟΝΟ[ ]
[ΚΟΝΔ]ΟΝΑΙΚΑΙΔΕΧΣΑΣ
_____[Ι]ΙΔΕΑΘΕΝΑΙ
_____[Ν]ΜΑΟΙΕΣΟΜ
_____ΙΝ_____ΙΟ
_____ΑΙ_____ΒΟΣ
_____ΣΟ___ΜΟΣ
_____ΕΘΑ
_____ΑΔΟ

```
_____EPI
_____MΠO
_____ENA
_____EE
_____ΣΘ
_____OΠ
```

Now housed in Athens' Epigraphical Museum, this inscription appears on a marble stele found between the Odeum and the Theatre of Dionysius (Tod 125). A relatively recent discovery of perhaps a century ago (Freeman 2. 617), there are several fragments of the inscription that remain unpublished (Hicks and Hill 91). This treaty is one example of efforts by Athens to ally with prominent cities in Sicily and Southern Italy to strengthen her position in Sicily and to undermine Syracuse's ever-increasing strength. Another such alliance was a treaty with Rhegium in the same year as the pact with Leontini that is now housed in the British Museum (*C.I.A.* i. 33; Hicks and Hill 90–91). The treaty with Leontini is particularly invaluable evidence in the history of rhetoric because it is a renewal of the alliance made before 433/2. This was the treaty Gorgias sought to implement in his famous embassy to Athens in 427 B.C. (Caven 20).

The treaty was formally proposed by Kallias (l. 15) and was presented with the formulaic language (1s. 1–3, 16–17) of a religious alliance ([Θε]οί . . χτσυμμαχίαν) with oaths "freely given" and "willingly accepted" (1s. 4, 18–19) between Athens and Leontini. All the relevant parties of Athens are listed as sanctioning the treaty: the Archon Aphseudos, the Prytaneis leader Akamantis, and Timoxsenos the President of the Boule or Assembly. As a counterpart, three ambassadors (literally, elders; 1s. 1–2) from Leontini (Πρέσβες ἐγ Λεον[τ]ίνον), stood in as representatives of their city: Timenor the son of Agathokleos, Sosis the son of Glaukios, and Gelon the son of Exsekestos (1s. 4–6).

The treaty provides the rationale for Athenian intervention should Syracuse again wage war with Leontini. This inscription offers evidence supporting the accuracy of Thucydides's account of the Leontini embassy to Athens (3. 86) as well as the rationale. It is clear that the mention of the embassy by Thucydides is based not only on the imminent war between Leontini and Syracuse but also on Athens' long-standing role in Sicily's political affairs. Thus,

Gorgias's embassy to Athens would have been not only welcomed but actually the expected result of careful manipulation to promote a democratic ally at a strategic point on a wealthy, sought-after island. Historians of rhetoric account for Gorgias's reputation in terms of his stylistic talents in rhetoric. It is equally clear that his skills extended to pragmatic, political talents which explain not only his trip to Athens but also his enormous success there as well.

Gorgias's trip to Athens in 427 B.C. was most likely taken in the role of elder or ambassador, entailing a great deal of responsibility and authority. In fact, Diodorus Siculus uses the same term (πρέσβεις) that appears in the treaty (l. 1) to describe the delegation that Gorgias headed in 427 B.C. (12. 53. 1–2). Despite the alliance, from 427–424 B.C., Syracuse besieged Leontini. Leontini sent its most famous rhetor, Gorgias, to solicit support for the agreement. Although Tisias was sent to represent Syracuse (Roberts), that city's strong affiliation with Corinth versus Leontini's affiliation with Athens made his mission almost impossible.

The embassy of 427 B.C. is often incompletely portrayed by historians of rhetoric as the occasion when rhetoric was "introduced" to the Athenians by Gorgias, who was a clear practitioner and teacher of the art. The political importance of the meeting, as this evidence reveals, is often ignored or down-played in favor of the artistic and intellectual merits of Gorgias's rhetoric. While Gorgias doubtlessly impressed his Athenian audience stylistically, it is also evident that he was effective (and popular) politically. Ambitious Athenian democrats may have recognized not only eloquence in Gorgias's rhetorical compositions but also a cogency in systematic argument that offered an excellent source of political power in a democracy.

Gorgias's embassy in 427 B.C. was a prelude to Athens' war with Syracuse and her disastrous defeat that began the decline of Athenian hegemony in the Greek world. Leontini, upon realizing the ineffectiveness of Athens against Syracuse, sued for peace and was granted citizenship status by Syracuse in 422 B.C. Syracuse's defeat of Athens in 415–413 B.C. signalled the end of Leontini's hope for independence. Ironically, the democracy of Syracuse that had enjoyed such gains fell to tyranny under Dionysius. A period lasting about two generations — spanning the lives of Corax, Tisias and Gorgias — witnessed rhetoric's emergence as a discipline within a political climate of democracy in Syracuse and Leontini. Transplanted to Athens during this period of democracy, rhetoric (again) prospered. The stability of democracy in Athens, however, was much more secure than in Syracuse. When democracy eroded, rhetoric experienced a loss of political effectiveness in Sicily. However, rhetoric was firmly entrenched in the political workings of Athenian life and the intellectual *paideia* of Athenian culture. While rhetoric's merits would be challenged on the grounds of its intellectual integrity and, indirectly, its power in political operations, it was by that time so endemic to the notion of democracy that any educational practices in a democracy would inherently presume the teaching of rhetoric. Gorgias's trip to Athens had done more than secure the political affiliations of two democracies; it had elevated rhetoric as an effective source of power within a democratic context.

Chapter *IV*

Significant Contributors to Sicilian Rhetoric

Empedocles and the Emergence of the Sicilian Sophistic

While the political climate in Sicily and Athens was a fertile environment for the growth of rhetoric, its development was also nurtured by continued intellectual and artistic activity. In a certain respect, sophists such as Gorgias were products of an intellectual movement grounded in the pragmatic belief that rhetoric could be developed into an effective system to use in political affairs. This Sicilian perspective toward rhetoric's development is best understood by examining the contributions of Empedocles, credited by Aristotle as "the one who invented rhetoric" (Diogenes Laertius 8. 57). A prominent pre-Socratic philosopher, Empedocles contributed significantly to rhetorical discourse. His views and use of style and the conceptual processes of antithetical thought driving it, the importance of relativism, sense-perception and probability were all synonymous with sophistic rhetoric. We will learn, however, that many of Empedocles' views were incompatible with Aristotelian rhetoric — despite Aristotle's belief that Empedocles "invented" rhetoric. Aristotle may have meant that Empedocles invented sophistic rhetoric, since he developed the foundation upon which it was based.

Platonic and Aristotelian Perspectives on Rhetoric's Origin

When Aristotle declared rhetoric to be the *antistrophos* (counterpart) of dialectic in the opening statement of his *Rhetoric*

57

(1354a; Grimaldi, 1980, 1–2), he challenged Plato's severance of rhetoric and philosophy which also excluded the evolution of the consciousness of discourse dating back to Homer. Plato's high regard for philosophy and disdain for sophistic rhetoric and poetic is readily apparent in *Gorgias, Phaedrus, Ion*, and *Republic* (see also several scholarly studies including Hunt; North; Erickson, 1980). Ironically, much of the confusion over the contributions of Empedocles and the sophists toward rhetoric are derived not from Plato's accounts—which are blatantly intolerant of any rhetoric which ignores Platonic Forms—but from Aristotle's restrictive view of rhetoric as essentially an explicit, rational process.

In the opening passage of his *Rhetoric*, Aristotle declared his opposition to earlier methods of rhetoric. He is responsible for a revolution in rhetorical thought precisely because he countered the non-rational, indirect methods of the sophistic with a rational system for the production of reasonable discourse. The theme of Aristotle's *Rhetoric* is that the pragmatic utility of rhetoric does not necessarily preclude it from being an intellectually rigorous techne. Aristotle's *Rhetoric* defined the province of the discipline more clearly than any other treatise. He elevated the status of deliberative, rational discourse by focusing on political rather than personal or artistic concerns, emphasizing invention and *pistis* (proof) over style and arrangement, highlighting *phronesis* (rational proof) and *krisis* (judgment), and designating rhetoric as a techne. These became the pivotal issues to redirect rhetoric's history. In his rapprochement of rhetoric and dialectic, however, Aristotle excluded other natural—and historical—relationships. While he establishes connecting links with philosophy, the thrust of the *Rhetoric* drives a wedge between rhetoric and poetry and summarily dismisses the sophistic movement as irrational.

Keith V. Erickson's essay (1976, 229–237) on Aristotle's earlier treatises on rhetoric even indicates that *Gryllus, Synagoge Technon* and *Theodectea* were essentially points of opposition, development and departure from sophistic rhetoric from which grew the ideas expressed in his *Rhetoric*. Although conciliatory references to prominent individuals such as Isocrates can be found in the *Rhetoric*, Aristotle had little respect for his contemporary rhetoricians or "technical writers" (1355a) as he referred to them. In fact, the opening of the *Rhetoric* explicitly reveals that Aristotle wrote the treatise as a salvo against sophistic rhetoric and wished his work to be set apart from past treatments. In the words of Theresa Crem (55), Aristotle did not wish to commit the "errors" of his predecessors. Scholars such as Chroust (37–51, esp. 44) and Erickson (1976, 230–232), who have studied the fragments of Aristotle's earlier work on rhetoric, the *Gryllus*, are univocal in their belief that it is an attack on earlier, sophistic rhetoric.

Evidently, Aristotle had strong, personal opposition to earlier treatments of rhetoric; in fact, he was so outraged by Isocrates' view that he believed that "it would be disgraceful to be silent" (Diogenes Laertius 5. 3; Quintilian 3. 1. 14; Cicero, *De Oratore* 3. 141). Cicero claimed in *De Oratore* (3. 141) that Aristotle actually "philosophized" his treatment of rhetoric because Isocrates' success was attained chiefly through style. Aristotle's *Rhetoric* may have been motivated by a desire to expose the spurious, nonintellectual treatments of rhetoric, but his statement also distorted what constituted rhetoric by disavowing earlier efforts as unworthy of being categorized within the province of his techne. Aristotle's attitude indicates his belief that sophistic techniques of composition were removed from rational thinking about rhetoric. Aristotle's view (*Rhetoric* 1354a, 1377b, 1378a; Arnhart 8, 12; Grimaldi, 1980, 349–356) was that the sophists and their predecessors were unconcerned with the nature of pistis (proof) and krisis (judgment), the direct rational system for the acquisition of probable truth. Aristotle's *Rhetoric*, as Book I reveals, is a preoccupation with heuristics (techniques for facilitating discovery and creativity). Heuristics drive discourse, utilize *topoi* (conceptual "places" or patterns of thinking), marshall style and dictate arrangement (*Rhetoric* 1355b). His concern with the nonformal rationality of rhetoric for political concerns is apparent in his praise of protreptic discourse — the language of philosophical deliberation — and his condemnation of eristic sophistic wrangling, producing only bantering rather than truth (*Rhetoric* 1371a, 1375a, 1377b, 1402a, 1414b; *Sophistici Elenchi* 183b–184a).

Both Plato's stringent criticism, and the legitimating thrust of Aristotle's *Rhetoric*, presented notions of rhetoric which dismissed or ignored sophistic contributions. Aristotle did not dismiss irrational rhetoric but rather nonrational rhetoric — rhetoric without an explicit techne or *ratio* (system). When Aristotle refused to acknowledge the nonrational aspects of rhetoric, he dismissed a long-established mode of expressing thoughts and sentiments and seriously tainted the sophistic movement. His characterization would continue uninterrupted for centuries afterwards. In short, Aristotle's *Rhetoric* portrays its discipline more as a revolution than an evolution in thought, more a departure from irrationality than an evolutionary step in the historical development of consciousness about discourse. Such a perspective is an imprecise accounting of pre-Aristotelian rhetoric. We will look at the precepts of Empedocles and criticisms of his work in an effort to determine sophistic contributions to Hellenic rhetoric. This examination should provide a more complete accounting of the notion of rhetoric indigenous to Hellenic thought than the dismissal by Plato and the characterization by Aristotle.

Empedocles: The "Inventor" of Sicilian Rhetoric

The Homeric, rhapsodic and logographic modes of discourse that preceded Empedocles did not offer an abstract system of heuristics but gave pre-eminence to poetic composition for the culmination of krisis and knowledge indirectly manifested through style and arrangement. Far from a rational system, the earliest notions of eloquent expression were believed to be grounded in divine inspiration and were modified over centuries by generations of composers who developed stylistic and formulaic constructions to create, preserve and transmit heroic tales. This attention to style and arrangement is understandable in early discourse, since ancient Greeks did not even begin to think of words in abstract isolation until the fifth century B.C. (Havelock, 1982, 8). In fact, it is the mark of the fifth century B.C. that abstraction of notions leading to a techne is made both conscious and explicit. For the centuries of Hellenic discourse prior to Corax and Tisias, stylistic techniques invented meaning. This apparent absence of systematization and diversification was noted by Aristotle (*Rhetoric* 1403b), who observed that the modes of composition which would eventually result in dramatic, lyric and historical composition had no real specialization. Such composers were often called poets, and it is understandable why, as Havelock notes (1982, 220–260, esp. 243), pre-Socratic philosophers such as Empedocles — in the tradition of his predecessors — composed treatises in lyrical verse.

Empedocles' works survive only in fragments and the scholia, or ancient commentaries, about his contributions are scattered throughout ancient literature and across centuries (D-K I, "31 [21]. Empedokles," 276–375). Synthesizing the evidence on Empedocles' contributions to rhetoric is a significant challenge, so much so that scholars such as George Kennedy (1963, 26, n. 1) believe that evidence on Empedocles' contributions is "unascertainable" and should therefore be ignored. Despite the difficulty, the knowledge gained about rhetoric is worth the effort.

Empedocles cannot properly be considered a sophist. Rather, he was a pre-Socratic philosopher; he belongs to the group of thinkers who initiated serious inquiry into the nature of the universe and mankind. Self-consciousness about man's abilities plus methods of structuring and acquiring knowledge were the foundation for sophistic rhetoric. Herein, we discover a key to understanding Empedocles' role as the inventor of rhetoric. Contrary to the observations of Kennedy mentioned above, the influences of Empedocles are ascertainable. The influence of this pre-Socratic philosopher on individuals such as Gorgias and possibly Tisias is generally recognized by scholars, who argue or imply a clear influence of Empedocles on early rhetoric (Untersteiner 6; Freeman, 1954, 92, ns. 5, 6; Roberts, 18 *et passim*; Diels, 1884, 343–368; Quintilian, 3. 1. 8. Freeman, 1966, 179). Empedocles himself was the pupil of Xenophanes, Anaxagoras, Parmenides and Pythagoras. More importantly, he was considered by Diogenes Laertius (8. 56, 57) to be a beneficiary of the Homeric tradition.

In a real sense, Empedocles bridges a gap between nonrational, divinely inspired Homeric discourse and the rational, systematic structuring of language which led to Aristotle's *Rhetoric* being viewed as revolutionary for producing discourse. As a beneficiary of a style of oratory grounded in meter, Empedocles utilized the hexameter and elegiac verse form characteristic of his Hellenic heritage, a "turgid and dithyrambic style" which Gorgias himself utilized in his sophistic rhetoric (Untersteiner, 93, 191). Empedocles' intellectual contributions grew out of poetic composition, his philosophical arguments are cast in hexameter and his methods of expressing thoughts and sentiments are grounded in such stylistic techniques as antithesis, metaphor, and analogy (Aristotle, *Poetics* 1447b; Freeman, 1954, 178; Kirk and Raven, 360; Untersteiner, 200; D-K I, 31[21]. B60; B148–151; Havelock, 1982, 200–260 (esp. 243).

Even a cursory reading of Plato's *Gorgias* immediately reveals that serious thinkers believed the use of stylistic procedures to sway listeners was both contemptible and irrational (see also, Aristotle, *Rhetoric* 1404a, 1408b). Yet, by using nonrational, indirect methods to move listeners. Gorgias was actually following a long tradition transmitted by his teacher Empedocles. Plato's (*Euthydemus* 277D-E; 278B-D; 282D; 288B,D,E; 289D-E; 290A; 307A-C; *Lysis* 211B; *Sophist* 225C, 231E) preference for protreptic discourse and disdain for eristic wrangling is even more pointed than Aristotle's (*Rhetoric* 1371a, 1375b, 1402a, 1414b; *Sophistici Elenchi* 183b-184a). Both believed that style was a necessary evil never to be emphasized since it fostered only the bantering characteristic of sophistic rhetoric (see also, Skousgaard, 379–380; Kustas, 48, 49, n. 2). Empedocles, then, is more rightly to be considered an inventor of rhetoric not in the Platonic or even Aristotelian sense, but rather in the earlier sophistic tradition which rivaled Aristotle's techne as a competing paradigm for centuries.

The methods by which Empedocles invented sophistic rhetoric are discernible both in his writings and in ancient commentaries about his efforts. While there are few concrete facts about Empedocles available, it is clear that he taught Gorgias and perhaps even Tisias, wrote his scientific and philosophical works in the florid Sicilian style and gave advice on rhetoric (Freeman, 1966, 177, 179; D-K 31[21]. A1 sec. 58; A2; A19; Diogenes Laertius 8. 53, 58). As was the case with his student Gorgias, Empedocles' style also was disparaged by Aristotle, who preferred the simple Attic dialect over the lofty embellishments synonymous with prominent non-Athenian sophists (D-K 31 [21]. A22; Untersteiner, 93; Aristotle, *Poetics* 1447b). A fair amount of this criticism is probably due to Empedocles' love of metaphor, which Aristotle believed to be a process incapable of being rationally understood and more appropriate to poetics than to rhetoric (*Rhetoric* 1405a; *Poetics* 1459a).

Empedocles' also employed antithesis frequently. Notions are syntactically structured through dissociation in such a manner that a *logos* (concept) is split into *dissoi logoi* and the idealization of a linear, directive process of rationality is eliminated and replaced by a paratactic (loosely organized) juxtaposition of notions (Untersteiner, 140). Aristotle so ardently opposed this intentional ambiguity as a rhetorical technique that he mocked the use of dissociation in verse form as comparable to having nothing to say and wishing only to hoodwink the public with beguiling style (*Rhetoric* 1407a, cf. 1410a-b). The poetic fragments of Empedocles, particularly *On Nature*, provide not only a physical explanation of the universe but also insights on how meaning can be synthesized through the counter-balancing of opposite notions. The fragments of Empedocles' work exude contradictory beliefs. While the presence of apparently incompatible positions has drawn criticism from scholars, the juxtaposition of antithetical concepts was more a correlative balancing of thesis and antithesis than intellectual inconsistency (Kirk and Raven, 322, 323). Empedocles' antithetical process was actually similar to the philosophical inquiry of the Pythagoreans and the paratactic method of Zeno (Aristotle, *Rhetoric* 1410a; Segal, 101, n. 18; Enos, 1976, 40–41).

Antithesis through *dissoi logoi* was more than a stylistic or even an intellectual formula for Empedocles; it was the foundation of his philosophical thought and central to Greek thought in general and sophistic thought in particular (Vernant, 122–123 [see the concept of "reciprocal opposition"]; Kerferd 5, 31–32 *et passim*). This method of knowing provides a major distinction between sophistic views and both Platonic and Aristotelian notions of rhetoric. In Aristotle's techne, syntactic cues of causal and co-existent notions are so clearly delineated that listeners follow an explicit, linear progression of thought rather than an antithetical counter-balancing of ideas associated with oral, poetic composition. Proponents of this view rejected discourse involving the structuring of opposites as encouraging indirection, relativism, and proportion. Since notions were not viewed as ontological and fixed (as in Platonic thought) but rather as synthesized and relative to the kairos or situation (Untersteiner 161; Kerferd 82), discourse predicated on the juxtaposition of notions was totally incompatible with discourse that claims a knowledge of essences not opposites. The distinction between Platonic logos and Empedoclean dissoi logoi are epistemologies in conflict; they are irreconcilable and would compel Plato to characterize such methods of coming-to-know as not true knowledge but only a false image of its appearance. Even the sophistic technique of *antilogos* (the prompting of dissociation by assigning the same logos with incompatible modifiers such as an individual being both wealthy and poor by relative standards) was treated with caution by Plato (Kerferd 61–65). Despite the close affinity of antilogos with dialectic, Plato believed that antilogos emphasized concerns of the phenomenal world rather than Platonic Forms and encouraged frivolous, eristic arguments (Kerferd 64–67). Thus, the essential methods Empedocles used to express his thoughts and sentiments — methods which were adopted by and integral to sophistic rhetoric — were opposed philosophically by Plato and rhetorically by Aristotle (Crem 55; Aristotle, *Rhetoric* 1354a–1355a; *Sophistici Elenchi* 183b, 184a). Lacking agreement on the starting points of rhetoric, both Plato and Aristotle would find little agreement with Empedocles and the sophists on either the nature or methods of rhetoric.

In addition to his mode of expression, Empedocles' views on

acquiring and gaining agreement about knowledge are in opposition to Platonic and Aristotelian thought but are the very nature of sophistic rhetoric. Where Plato believed that the senses were inaccurate and limited in acquiring knowledge, Empedocles believed that awareness through sense-perception was the only legitimate way of coming-to-know: a concept which sophists readily accepted (Untersteiner, 154–159; Sextus Empiricus, *adversus Mathematicos* 7. 125; Levi, 24–25 [this reference is cited in Untersteiner, 155, ns. 83–84]; Theophrastus, *De Sensu* 7). Empedocles' views on sense-perception were grounded in the belief that knowledge can only be communicated through sense-awareness. Since man's senses are finite, and thus complete communication is unattainable, man's very existence necessitates a system of probability which is filtered through the "pores" of his senses (Untersteiner, 158–159; Theophrastus, *De Sensu* 7). Empedocles' view of sense-perception precluded the possibility of perceiving and communicating with the gods — who were beyond the reality of human senses (Clemens Alexandrinus, *Stomateis* 5. 81. 2). From this perspective, there is no division of logic and emotion that warrants the analogy of the charioteer in Plato's *Phaedrus* — the horse of reason pulling man up to the heavens, the horse of passion dragging him down to the earth. Rather, for Empedocles, emotion and logic are inextricably bound (and limited) by sense-awareness.

Empedocles could justly be viewed as the inventor of rhetoric, for his views on communication stressed man and probability rather than gods and myth — a marked departure from his Homeric tradition and a cornerstone for sophistic rhetoric. Empedocles' view that knowledge is acquired through the senses and limited by perception led him to consider the mind as only another agent for perception (D-K 31 [21]. A86; Theophrastus, *De Sensu* 10; Untersteiner, 156, n. 87). The power of speech, however, is that it can so deceive the senses that words can stimulate reactions as though they were actual events. This approach was an anathema to such "serious thinkers" as Plato (e. g. *Gorgias* and *Phaedrus*) and Aristotle (*Rhetoric* 1404a) — who tried to strip away or disparage emotive response from rhetoric. Yet, for Empedocles and the sophists who followed him, it represented a way of knowing consistent with the history of Greek thought. As Havelock notes, "sophists, pre-Socratics, and Socrates" were all "trying to discover and to practice abstract thinking" (1963/1982), 286). Unlike Socrates, Plato, and Aristotle, the sophists and pre-Socratics closely identified with their oral, poetic heritage and assimilated emotivism into their understanding of rhetoric rather than severing the connection (Kerferd, 24). For Plato, knowledge could never be reduced to a condition where intelligence co-existed with perception and where probability was given deference over unattainable certainty. While Empedocles embraced the nonrational processes of discourse, Plato and Aristotle drove a wedge between rational and emotional processes — idealizing the former and characterizing the latter as a necessary evil.

The Legend of Corax and Tisias

The Coherence of Ancient Sources

Although there is a range of interpretation over the particular activities and influence of Corax and Tisias, our most prominent ancient sources provide a generally consistent view of Corax, Tisias and their students. Later in the chapter, we will see that far less agreement exists about specific contributions. However, we can learn a great deal by looking at the areas of agreement and disagreement.

In *Sophistici Elenchi*, Aristotle discusses the origins of rhetoric and the tradition that preceded him (183B), acknowledging the existence of a discipline he would chronicle in his lost *Synogoge Technon* (Cicero, *De Inventione* 2.2.6; Erickson 1976). While Aristotle recognizes Tisias as an early figure in rhetoric's development, he clearly states that Tisias followed rhetoric's originators (πρώτους) (183B). Tisias, Aristotle further tells us, was himself succeeded by Thrasymachus, Theodorus, and many others after them (183B). This view of Tisias as a member of a line of succession is confirmed by Pausanias, who saw Tisias as one who "improved" the art of rhetoric (*Elis* 2. 17. 8). Aristotle's *Rhetoric* mentions Corax in a similar manner (2. 24. 11), as does the unknown author of the *Rhetorica Ad Alexandrum*, who claimed that Corax wrote a techne (1421B).

Lesser-known ancient authorities, fragmentary accounts from prominent authorities and scholiasts, and late Hellenistic and Byzantine scholars provide further information about the contributions and activities of Corax and Tisias and the founding of rhetoric on Sicily. The collection of ancient sources contained in Radermacker's *Artium scriptores* and Waltz's collection of later Hellenic scholars, *Rhetores Graeci*, provide information that is generally consistent despite a few conflicting details. Most of these latter authorities agree that Corax and Tisias were responsible for the formalization and teaching of rhetoric in Syracuse and the spread of rhetoric to other cities in Sicily, Athens and eventually the Hellenic world. Some of these ancient scholars debate whether the impact of Corax and Tisias' rhetoric began in the law courts or the assembly. Of particular interest in these latter collections are the comments of Doxopatros, Sopatros, Troilos, and a work referred to as the *Prolegomena*. They emphasize the pragmatic utility of rhetoric in meeting the needs of the people of Syracuse and Sicily in general. Both the *Prolegomena* of Hermogenes and the *Prolegomena* of Troilos, for example, discuss the role that Corax played in the transition of Syracuse from a tyranny to a democracy. In fact, the *Prolegomena* of Hermogenes offers the possible interpretation that Corax may have been an advisor to the king before Syracuse's (brief) transformation to democracy. If this ancient commentary is accurate, the transformation of his rhetoric from the power of a tyrant to the pragmatics of a democracy was living evidence of the role of rhetoric changing from courtly, advised expression to a skill essential to effective discourse in the democratic concerns of law and politics.

These later Greek authorities often emphasize the deliberative benefits of rhetoric to the community (*demos*) through particular achievements, with a high degree of sensitivity to political and social conditions, that explain the context for the growth and spread of rhetoric. Doxopatros, as well as other later Greek scholars, discussed the long-standing alliance and cultural ties between Athens and Leontini that help explain Gorgias's reception in Athens. There is a general consistency to the social accounts of Corax, Tisias and the conditions on Sicily to provide some support for the accuracy of rhetoric's emergence as a discipline on Sicily. None of these latter sources directly refutes the earlier ancient sources. Contemporary scholars debate the particulars, but we should not let those disagreements blind us to the general historical accuracy of the role of Corax and Tisias in developing rhetoric into a formal discipline.

The testimony of these sources provide a reasonably clear picture about the origins of rhetoric as a discipline. There is no doubt that Tisias existed; the confirmation of several independent sources and historical artifacts makes that point certain. The references to Corax as his mentor have been disputed by contemporary scholars but their views offer no counter-evidence, only skepticism. The historical period in which Tisias lived is so well documented that the possibility that his mentor of the preceding generation was only a myth is highly unlikely. On the contrary, the consistency of ancient sources confirming the existence of Corax does more than perpetuate a legend, it reinforces the possibility of Corax's activities to the degree that they become credible.

Other well known ancient scholars not only confirm the existence of Corax and Tisias but even mention individual students. Dionysius of Halicarnassus records that Lysias, a prominent logographer in Athens mentioned in Plato's *Phaedrus*, was born in Syracuse and taught by Tisias (*Lysias* 1) along with Isocrates, who studied with both Tisias and Gorgias (*Isocrates* 1). Plutarch confirms Lysias' Syracusian heritage and study under Tisias (*Moralia* 835C,D) and reaffirms his strong connection with Sicily and Isocrates, whom Plutarch also says studied under Gorgias and Tisias (*Moralia* 836F). As did Aristotle, Dionysius of Halicarnassus and Plutarch provide evidence of a tradition of rhetoric in which Corax and Tisias were early practitioners as well as evidence of interaction among Leontini, Syracuse, and Athens.

As with their earlier counterparts, later Greek scholars and Roman rhetoricians shared much the same view of rhetoric's origin. As a youth of about nineteen, Cicero at first thought that Tisias was the founder of rhetoric (*De Inventione* 2. 2. 6). In his more mature works, Cicero readily acknowledges Corax as rhetoric's founder (*De Oratore* 1. 20. 91; *Brutus* 12. 46). Cicero had access to works of rhetoric that are now lost; perhaps his later exposure to these works convinced him that Corax was rhetoric's founder. Quintilian confirms Cicero's view of Corax and Tisias as the originators of rhetoric in the *Institutio oratoria* (2. 17. 7). Quintilian also acknowledges the belief that Corax and Tisias wrote technai and mentions that Empedocles was the first to recognize rhetoric as a study (3. 1. 8), a view shared by Sextus Empiricus, who saw Empedocles as the one who "cultivated" (κεκινηκέναι) rhetoric (*Against the Logicians* 1. 6). Sextus Empiricus, however, clearly recognized Corax as a prominent, early figure (Against the Professors 2. 96).

Such remarks make it apparent that one criterion for becoming established in a discipline (or, for that matter, establishing a discipline) of rhetoric is to write a techne, for our sources all credit Corax, Tisias and Gorgias as early figures in rhetoric's formation as a discipline because they wrote technai. Plato recognized Tisias as not only a prominent early figure in rhetoric but one who popularized the study of probability (*Phaedrus* 267A,B) in both Sicily and Athens (*Phaedrus* 273A–274A)—doubtlessly when he went to Athens with Gorgias of Leontini in 427 B.C. to discuss the Athenian alliance treaty (Pausanias, *Elis* 2. 17. 8).

Information from prominent figures of antiquity, ones regularly drawn upon to substantiate historical accuracy in rhetoric, further help to unravel the legend of Corax and Tisias and to place other figures, such as Polus, who appear or are mentioned in such works as Plato's *Gorgias* and *Phaedrus*. It is generally accepted that Empedocles first invented the possibility of rhetoric as a discipline, largely because of his views on language, sense perception, relativism and probability. Corax, however, wrote a techne systematizing rhetoric and was thus credited as its "founder." Tisias, his fellow Syracusan was a student of Corax and eventually an educator whose published techne became well known. Gorgias, himself the student of Tisias and possibly Corax, also published a techne. He too became a distinguished educator. Both Tisias and Gorgias went to Athens and attracted prominent students, some of the most well known in the history of rhetoric—Lysias, Polus and Isocrates. In fact, and by way of completing the cycle, Wilcox has observed that Isocrates may have been the teacher of Timaeus, who is one of the ancient sources used to reconstruct these early developments (1943 23). These second-generation educators also helped to spread the Sicilian sophistic. These later sophists extended the reach of rhetoric throughout the Hellenic world. Lysias became a famous logographer in Athens, Gorgias travelled extensively and Polus opened a school of rhetoric in Southern Italy at Thurii. In approximately four generations, rhetoric evolved from a notion with Empedocles, to a formalized techne with Corax and Tisias, to an established discipline through the activities of sophists such as Gorgias, logographers such as Lysias, orators such as Antiphon, and educators such as Isocrates. Rhetoric was planted in Sicily, spread from there to Athens, and eventually throughout the Hellenic world.

What may be unclear is precisely how these major figures of early rhetoric relate. If we can better understand the relationship of these major figures to one another, we can have a better picture of which ideas were most likely transmitted. Our understanding of ancient sources enables us to trace their relationship in the following manner.

Pythagoras Samos/Croton (So. Italy)

Eleatics: Parmenides and Zeno Elea (So.Italy)

Empedocles Acragas (Sicily)

Corax Syracuse (Sicily)

Tisias Syracuse (Sicily)

Gorgias Leontini (Sicily)

Thrasymachus (Chalcedon)

[Theodorus]

Lysias (Sicily)/Athens

Polus Agrigentum (Sicily)   **Isocrates** Athens

Timaeus (Sicily)

Possible Influences Shaping Sophistic Rhetoric

1. oppositional thoughts/contradictions
2. sense perception
3. relativism/opinion
4. dialectic
5. oral composition/poetic formulae
6. literacy

_____ = direct influence

- - - - - - = possible, indirect or lesser influence

The Incoherence of Current Scholarship

To state that there is current disagreement over the particular contributions, benefits and even the very existence of Corax and Tisias is an understatement. Current scholarship questions whether the activities of Corax and Tisias should be called rhetoric and even whether Corax existed. Thomas Cole is the strongest proponent of the belief that Corax never existed (22–27, 82), and Edward Schiappa argues convincingly that rhetoric was not even mentioned as a discipline during the time of Corax and Tisias (49–54). Cole's view flies in the face of centuries of ancient testimony and is certainly subject to argument. Schiappa's point about rhetoric as a discipline, however, is very well made and worthy of note. In *Protagoras and Logos*, Schiappa presents a fine summary of current scholarship on Corax and Tisias. Current work, as Schiappa shows, is limited and inconsistent, for scholars range from accepting the invention of rhetoric by Corax and Tisias as an uncontested starting point to various works citing qualifications and uncertainties. While it may well be true, as Schiappa argues, that activities, systems and even technai were not formally named rhetoric, it is clear that the immediately succeeding generations, including Aristotle and Plato, perceived what Corax and Tisias did as rhetoric. Schiappa is certainly correct in recognizing the lack of a named and proclaimed discipline but we should also recognize those individuals and contributions that provided the basis for rhetoric. Another important point is one that has been emphasized here repeatedly. Current scholarship is inherently a-contextual; it does not provide a grounding in the context in which these activities occurred. The social and political forces are vitally important ingredients in piecing together the likelihood of the contributions of Corax and Tisias to the evolution of rhetoric as a discipline.

Debate over particulars dominate present-day scholarship on Corax and Tisias. George Kennedy has argued that "there is no evidence to indicate that any Hellenistic rhetoricians regarded the history of rhetoric as beginning before the time of Corax and Tisias" (1957 31–32). Yet, we have seen that forces leading to the development of rhetoric were in operation for centuries prior to Corax and Tisias. Scholarship over the last one hundred years, accepting the ancient view that the start of the study of rhetoric should begin with Corax and Tisias, has all but ignored this pre-history, choosing rather to refine previous knowledge and accepted interpretations. Our efforts at understanding this preliminary period, however, enables us to have a more sensitive understanding of views about Corax and Tisias.

Current efforts have been directed toward revealing inconsistencies over the historical accounting of Corax, Tisias and, subsequently, the evolution of rhetoric into a discipline. The compilation of ancient fragments during the nineteenth and twentieth centuries has made apparent that some ancient sources did in fact offer incompatible accounts of Corax and Tisias. While a few current scholars, such as Cole, are skeptical over the very existence of Corax (24), most modern scholars do not dispute the existence of Corax and none question the legitimacy of Tisias as an historical figure. Much of the debate about Corax, as captured so well by Wilcox (1942, 1943), centers on whether his emphasis in Syracuse was primarily in legal rhetoric or political rhetoric. Another controversy in the legend of Corax and Tisias has centered on their relationship. Most scholars agree that Corax predated Tisias slightly. Some, such as Kennedy (1959, 177) claim that they actually had no close relationship, while Verral argued that they quite possibly were co-authors of the first Hellenic techne of rhetoric (1880 197). Greek scholars, writing as much as several centuries after the period, have provided valuable but inconsistent information. Most credited Corax with formalizing a theory of probability, but specifics over his contributions and his divisions of rhetorical argument into parts range widely. Some, in fact, credit his scheme of arrangement as ranging from 3, 4 and 7 parts (Wilcox 1943) to 5 (Verral). The inaccuracies of Hellenistic scholars such as Sopater have caused some authorities such as Wilcox to encourage current researchers to "disregard" such accounts as "worthless" (1943 14).

Although it is frustrating to reconcile dissimilar historical accounts, the inclination to dismiss these sources out of hand should be avoided. While it is true that the particulars of Corax and Tisias's activities may be difficult to reconstruct, there is also — on another level — amazing consistency over the important, major factors related to rhetoric's evolution into a discipline prior to Aristotle. It is clear from contemporaneous ancient sources, later Hellenistic accounts and the research of scholars over the last two centuries, that some evidence persists. Before we accept the most skeptical arguments of recent scholars, we should reiterate these points. Most authorities (past and present) recognize the existence of Corax and Tisias. The certainty of Tisias's existence, and the close chronological sequencing of events with Corax, makes the possibility of Corax's existence extremely probable. It would seem almost nonsense to create a mythological Corax who would be only a few years older than the very real Tisias. Second, the historical events in Sicily (particularly in Syracuse) and Athens are so thoroughly documented that the events themselves emphasize the conditions which prompted and nurtured the popularization and formalization of rhetoric for very pragmatic reasons. As we have discussed, treaties between Athens and Leontini add weight to the accuracy of those conditions. Third, our expanding knowledge of the period teaches us that the rhetoric of Corax and Tisias would probably not have been so specialized that we need to be deeply concerned about it. Even at the nascent stage, rhetoric would have adapted as easily to legal proceedings as it would have to popular, political persuasion. In fact, one of the most consistent markers of rhetoric throughout its rich history has been its adaptability, and there is no reason to think that this range would not have existed even in incipient stages. Rhetoric did come to the mind of Sicilians as a techne unto itself. When Gorgias came to Athens, he viewed himself not only as an ambassador of Leontini but as a sophist. While no one argues that practical, pragmatic discourse was used in public affairs of cities such as Athens long before Gorgias arrived, it is also evident that his visit there increased attention to rhetoric. In addition to model orations, more abstract and theoretical notions about rhetoric were introduced to the consciousness of a discipline in formation.

Gorgias: The "Father" of the Sicilian Sophistic

The biased characterization of Gorgias of Leontini in Plato's famous dialogue was a gross misrepresentation of one of the most innovative theorists in Greek rhetoric. The temptation to use the *Gorgias* as a factually definitive and credible historical source has resulted in misunderstanding the real man. Plato's dialogue was so distorted that Gorgias himself denied that he ever uttered any of the lines attributed to him in the *Gorgias*, dismissing Plato's work as a humorous satire (Athenaeus 11. 505 D,E). Nevertheless, the acceptance of Plato's dialogue has encouraged the notion that Gorgias's main contributions to rhetoric were stylistic devices, a belief overshadowing and distorting other contributions which Gorgias made to rhetorical theory and argument.

The major assault upon Gorgias has been directed toward his

intellectual contributions and philosophical convictions. Mario Untersteiner (201–202) and E. R. Dodds (7) indicate that several scholars view Gorgias as neither a philosopher nor even a sophist, but maintain instead that Gorgias can only be considered a rhetor. Both ancient (Isocrates, *Antidosis* 268–269, *Helen* 3; Xenophon, *Memorabilia* i. 1. 14 ff.; Sextus Empiricus, *Against the Professors* 7. 65 ff.) and modern (H. Gomperz, 1–35; Loenen, 201–202; Kennedy, 1963, 182) scholars have characterized Gorgias as merely a glib nihilist who advanced no positive theories and was unconcerned with ethics. Even Gorgias's famed discourse has come under severe criticism. George Kennedy asserts that Gorgias is not a prominent figure in the history of rhetoric and reduces his contributions to poetic devices (1963, 33), a view supported by other prominent thinkers (Aristotle, *Rhetoric* 1404A24; Philostratus, *Vitae Sophistarum* 492–493; Diodorus Siculus 12.53). W. Rhys Roberts argues that Gorgias wrote no formal rhetorical treatise (τέχνη) and that his oratory emphasized trivial matters with "claptrap" strategies (18–19; see also Isocrates, *Helen* 3, 4).

Contemporary writers in various disciplines, however, have come to regard Gorgias as a serious thinker and have encouraged a thorough study of his views. Charles Segal (1962), for example, has shown that Gorgias's observations reveal a concern for psychological inquiry. While Segal did not stress the implications of Gorgian thought for rhetoric itself, researchers in speech communication have promoted a re-examination of Gorgias as an important contributor to rhetorical theory. Everett Lee Hunt, who built upon the pioneer efforts of Bromley Smith, made scholars of rhetoric aware that Gorgias was "a participant in the philosophical controversies of his time" (29). The early research of Smith and Hunt was significantly advanced by Bruce E. Gronbeck (1972), who provided the first in-depth examination of Gorgias's thoughts on rhetoric and poetic. Gronbeck's contribution centered upon identifying and describing the major tenets of Gorgian thought, which had previously been considered only in philology and philosophy. The reconstruction of Gorgias's philosophical perspective on rhetoric by Gronbeck prompted further inquiry by Richard A. Engnell (1973) who argued that many of Gorgias's concerns in "rhetorical epistemology" are still serious concerns of contemporary communication theorists. Such research has not resolved conflicting evaluations of Gorgias's contributions to rhetoric, but it has demonstrated the need to reassess the fragments of Gorgias's work through a critical examination of the actual Greek texts. Gorgias made significant contributions to rhetoric prior to Aristotle and may even be considered the "father" of the Sicilian Sophistic. We have already seen the role Gorgias played in the relationship between the cities of Leontini, Syracuse and Athens. An examination of biographical information complementing what we already know of Gorgias from earlier sections of this book, along with a critical examination of his extant fragments, will provide clues to the intellectual forces which influenced Gorgias's view of rhetoric.

Intellectual Influences on Gorgian Rhetoric

Gorgias was born in Leontini, the son of a man named Charmantides. Although his birthdate is uncertain, scholars have agreed upon a date no earlier than (and probably some years after) 500 B.C. (Pausanias 6. 2. 17; Freeman, 1966, 354). Several ancient scholars (Diodorus Siculus 12. 53; Pausanias 6. 2. 117; Philostratus 494) have helped to pinpoint important dates in Gorgias's life, and it is virtually certain that Gorgias was near seventy-three years old when he first visited Athens in 427 B.C., and may have lived to be as old as 108. Despite the seminal influence upon rhetoric which modern scholars credit to Corax and Tisias, Gorgias was not only considered the "father of sophists" by ancient authorities (Philostratus 492; Pausanias 6. 2. 17) but the first individual to "revive" the study of rhetoric. Corax, Tisias, and Gorgias were all figures of major importance in Sicilian rhetoric; yet, the Sicilian historian Diodorus (12. 53–54; cf. Roberts, 18, c.2; Hinks, 66 ff.) clearly ranks Gorgias above his contemporaries. In fact, when Gorgias and Tisias led their respective embassies in 427 B.C. to petition the Athenians to mediate the dispute between Syracuse and Leontini, Pausanias claims that Gorgias easily won the Athenian alliance by his persuasive prowess (6.2.17). However, as our discussion earlier in the book makes clear, Athens' established treaty and strong cultural ties with Leontini doubtlessly enhanced Gorgias's position.

Beyond his oratorical ability, Gorgias was esteemed as an educator. There is evidence supported by Dionysius of Halicarnassus and others (*De compositione verborum* 12, p. 84 in D-K 82. B13; Aristotle, *Sophistici Elenchi* 183B34–41, *Rhetoric* 1419B3; Plato, *Phaedrus* 261B; Gerke, 341–344; cf. Untersteiner, 96, ns. 76–80; Guthrie, *The Sophists*, 44, 192–193) that Gorgias wrote a treatise on rhetoric. In any event, Gorgias was regarded as the foremost sophist and, like Protagoras, he amassed great wealth from teaching (Diodorus Siculus 12. 53; Athenaeus 3. 113E; Plato, *Apologia* 19 D,E). Unlike Protagoras and other sophists, however, Gorgias never claimed to teach virtue (arete), the ideal of intellectual excellence (Plato, *Meno* 95C; Jaeger II, 369–370). Despite his high fees, Gorgias attracted a considerable number of prestigious students (Diodorus Siculus 12. 53; Xenophon, *Anabasis* 2. 16, *Symposium* 1. 5; Philostratus 497), the most famous of whom was Isocrates. Gorgias's students rank among the most prominent intellectual figures of fifth-century B.C. Greece: Polus of Agrigentum, the dialogue-character in Plato's *Gorgias* (Philostratus, 13); Alcidamus of Elaea, who took over Gorgias's school in Athens (Aristotle, *Rhetoric* 1406B; D-K 82. A2; Freeman, *The Pre-Socratic Philosophers*, 356); and the famous Boetian general, Proxenus, who studied statesmanship under Gorgias (Xenophon, *Anabasis* 2. 6. 17). The eminent philosopher Antisthenes was a student of Gorgias before he turned to Socrates (Diogenes Laertius 6. 2.).

Acknowledgement of Gorgias's mastery of stylistic devices, σχήματα Γοργίεια (Athenaeus 504E; Xenophon, *Symposium* 2. 26), complemented the acclaim which he received in Athens and at Olympian assemblies for his oratory and indicates that Gorgias literally practiced what he preached (Norden; Philostratus 492–493). In contrast to Plato's carpings in the *Gorgias* and *Phaedrus* and Aristotle's criticisms (*Rhetoric* 1406B), Gorgias was admired and respected by such prominent individuals as Thucydides, Pericles, Aspasia, Critias, Alcibiades and Agathon (D-K 84. A9; Freeman, *The Pre-Socratic Philosophers*, 356; Philostratus 493).

About a century after Gorgias began to teach rhetoric in Athens, Aristotle wrote his *Rhetoric* and began by claiming that rhetoric has its counterpart in dialectic. Aristotle's view on the relationship of rhetoric and dialectic was preceded by Gorgias and earlier Greek thinkers. Empedocles and Zeno, the respective inventors of rhetoric and dialectic, both influenced the system of argument (Aristotle, *Rhetoric* 1354A; Diogenes Laertius 8. 57) promoted by Gorgias. As a student of Empedocles, Gorgias was not only exposed to a dominant pre-Socratic philosophy but also to a pre-Socratic rhetoric. As we learned earlier, Empedocles inherited a form of oratory bound by meter (λόγον ἔχουτα μέτρου), a style which Gorgias clearly utilized (Untesteiner 93, 191). The style was a direct descendant from a Homeric, poetic tradition (Segal 120, n. 85; Gorgias, *Helen*

2). The rhetorical contributions which Empedocles transmitted to his student Gorgias outstripped mere poetic verse, for Empedocles demonstrated an intellectual as well as a stylistic development. As we have discussed, the fragments of Empedocles' work frequently juxtaposed antithetical concepts—in the tradition of the philosophical inquiry of the Pythagoreans and the dichotomous method of Zeno. The method was so familiar to Aristotle (*Rhetoric* 1410A22) that it was considered a characteristic of both Sicilian and Southern Italian philosophical schools (Segal 101, 18n; Untersteiner 200, 39n and 40n). The notion of contraries, however, was more than a stylistic formula for Gorgias; it was the conceptual foundation of his rhetoric.

Empedocles' principle of verification rested with human sense-perception. In a marked departure from the cautious skepticism of his teacher Parmenides (Sextus Empiricus, *adversus Mathematicos* 7. 125), Empedocles stressed an anthropocentric worldview which placed trust not with the gods but with human senses—a concept which Gorgias readily accepted (Levi 24–25; Untersteiner 155, 83n and 84n). Man's ability to acquire knowledge—and for that matter, to perceive existence itself—was dependent upon the degree of his sense-perception (Theophrastus, *De sensu* 7). Since man's capacity for understanding reality was finite, complete communication was impossible and required a system of probability which was limited by sensory experience (Untersteiner 158–159; Theophrastus, *De sensu* 7). As a student of Empedocles, Gorgias accepted his teacher's concept of sense-reality and its implications for communication (Plato, *Meno* 76C; Lamb 284–285, 1n and 2n; Diogenes Laertius 8. 58; D-K 82. A2, 3, 10). It remained for Gorgias, however, to develop these kernel concepts into a highly sophisticated system of rhetoric.

In order to understand Gorgias's view of rhetoric it is necessary, as [Aristotle] advises, to examine the views of other philosophers who influenced him (*De Melisso, Xenophane, Gorgia* 980B). [Aristotle] credited much of Gorgian philosophy to concepts which were initially articulated by the pre-Socratic philosophers Melissus, Zeno and Parmenides, Zeno's and Empedocles' instructor (979A). Diogenes Laertius (8. 56), however, qualifies the influence which Parmenides had on Empedocles and implies that Xenophanes had a stronger impact on Empedocles' notions of sense-perception and probability ([Aristotle] 977A ff.; D-K 31. A7; Kirk and Raven 320, 411n; Simplicius, *Aristotelis de Physica Commentarii* 25. 19). Parmenides argued that there are only two avenues for securing knowledge or understanding (D-K 28. B2; Guthrie, *A History of Greek Philosophy*, II, 13–14). The first requires the use of persuasion for the sake of approaching truth. The second avenue is to avoid inquiry into matters that are nonexistent. Communication is impossible about such matters because of the lack of tangible references that can be communicated through the senses (D-K 28, B2, 3). For Parmenides, understanding is perceived through the senses but judged and evaluated through man's reason or logos (D-K 28. B7). Therefore, sensory and mental limitations prohibit humans from ever acquiring certain knowledge (D-K 28. B6). Generations later, Plato would oppose Parmenides' position, arguing that "irrational" sensation inhibits man's reasoning powers and his quest for truth (*Timaeus* 27D; *Phaedo* 65A–66A). Unlike Plato, Parmenides believed that the limited capacity of the human mind and the inherent deception (a concept of Gorgias's which will be discussed later) in communication precluded absolute certainty of the existence of real truths and compelled a way of knowing based on probability and opinion (D-K 28. B8. 50–61)—a view Gorgias would bring to his rhetoric.

Gorgias was the beneficiary not only of the theory of probability but also of a philosophical tradition that would establish tenets for support of his anti-Platonic view of rhetoric. A generation before Gorgias, Zeno formalized the notion of securing contrary conclusions from shared premises and established the dialectical method of arguing from contrary positions (Diogenes Laertius 8. 57, 9. 25; Plato *Sophista* 216A, *Phaedrus* 261D; Aristotle, *Rhetoric* 1355A-B, *Topica* ff.). This system of inquiry proceeds from premises that are not agreed upon; the conclusions result in a choice of probable positions. Thus, contrary to the dialectic of Plato (*Parmenides* 128A; *Phaedrus* 261 D,E ff.), conclusions expose contradictory positions in relative degrees of strength. The apparent incompatibility of these paradoxical and antithetical positions prompted Plato to dismiss such notions as avoiding a quest for absolute knowledge (*Phaedrus* 261D) and attempting to confuse appearance with reality. Plato's objection to the philosophical implications of Gorgias's rhetoric concentrated upon the charge that such inquiries did not seek knowledge as a realization of virtue (*Gorgias* 455A). Consequently, the inherent worth of rhetoric could in no way compare with that of the "art" of philosophy, which avoids deception and seeks truth (*Phaedrus* 262B,C) by examining knowledge of first principles (*Phaedrus* 272D). Plato saw an unbridgeable gap between the examination of certain knowledge leading to virtue and the "deception" inherent in the relativism of sophistic rhetoric.

Gorgias's philosophical opinions on the nature of existence and non-existence, knowledge and probability, and antithesis and deception derived from inquiry conducted long before Socrates or Plato developed their respective positions on rhetoric. In opposing Socrates' views, Gorgias was not (as Plato would have us believe in the *Gorgias*) being "unphilosophical," he was presenting an antithetical view of rhetoric which was nourished through the teaching of Empedocles, the Eleatics, and other intellectuals from Sicily and Southern Italy.

The Epistemology of Gorgias's Rhetoric

One of Plato's major criticisms of Gorgias was his concern for probability rather than "truth" (ἀλήθεια). For Plato, Gorgias's system of antithetical reasoning emphasized probability and opinion so predominantly that the truth or falsehood of a principle seemed to be altogether arbitrary (*Phaedrus* 267A,B and 272D). The antithetical nature of Gorgias's persuasion is illustrated clearly in the fragments of his *Epitaphios* (D-K 82. B6; see also, Gorgias, *Palamedes* 9, 22 and *Helen*: 8). In this oration, Gorgias demonstrates an ability to structure a hierarchy of values for his listeners by dissociating the following notions: tempered reason and stringent justice; mind and body; thinking and doing; helpers and rebukers; violence and restraint; and courage and terror. The persuasiveness in Gorgias's epideictic oratory derives from his ability to elevate the proper course of action by stylistically illustrating the antithetical, cowardly behavior rejected by heroic warriors who died in battle. Through the portrayal of the diametrically opposed choices confronting the warriors, the listeners might gain an insight into the implications of valor.

Plato's criticism fails to recognize Gorgias's view of rhetoric predicated on dissociated concepts (δισσοὶ λόγοι) (Untersteiner 179; Cicero, *Brutus* 46, 47; Diodorus Siculus 12. 53. 4). Plato believed that ideas had an immutable nature which, when discovered, would reveal certain knowledge. Gorgias believed, however, that knowledge was revealed by understanding the dichotomies inherent in the nature of individual concepts. Thus, the nature of rhetoric depends upon the proportion of "truthfulness" or "falsehood" it exhibits at any given time. The foundation for such a position can be found in the Pythagorean philosophy of opposites, which argues that the universe functions through a synthetic and harmonious proportion of opposites (Untersteiner 120, 86n; Aristotle, *Rhetoric* 1410A). Untersteiner demonstrates the dynamic nature of this rhetoric while quoting Pythagoras, "καιρός [balance] and its allied concept δίκαιον [justice] 'then found their application in the relations and communications between man and man, communications which are bound to vary according to age and office and kinship and state of mind'" (Untersteiner 110).

For Gorgias, understanding the nature of a thing meant understanding the circumstances and dissociated forces that created it — the degree and proportion of dissimilar energies which resulted in a particular phenomenon. With such an epistemology, the perceived appearance depends upon a balance of dissociated concepts (δισσοὶ λόγοι) based upon perceived appearance. Gorgias actually taunted his accusers for their lack of factual certainty, a type of empirical knowledge, in his *Palamedes* (5, 22–24; see also, Aristotle, *Rhetoric* 1402A; Plato, *Phaedrus* 273A-E). The dissociation of concepts could not occur without deception; that is, words had to appear to be synonymous with experiences actually perceived and not their mere symbolic representation. "For," as Gorgias argued, "that which is communicated is speech, but speech is not that which is perceived by the senses and actually exists; therefore the things that actually exist, which are observed, are not communicated but [only] speech, but they are perceived by the senses" (D-K 82. B3. 84; recorded in Sextus Empiricus, *Against the Professors* 7. 84–86). Gorgias's rhetoric stressed an antithesis which went beyond the stylistic form that earned him distinction to reveal and direct a philosophical method of inquiry. Moreover, the dissociation of concepts often advanced the negative, which is inherently nonexistent and thus lacks a specific referent. In order to structure antithetical relationships, listeners had to be "deceived" into providing meaning for notions which did not come from sensory experience.

Deception for Gorgias meant the artificial creation of sensory experiences through the power of evocative words and the practice of advancing antithetical arguments for the sake of securing probable conclusions. Yet, as Gorgias cautioned, when used with harmful intent, persuasion can drug and beguile the soul (4). Gorgias's clearest statement on the place of deception in rhetorical theory is in his *Helen* (D-K 82. B11. 1–21.). He believed that one of the virtues of speech was its power to reveal the nature of situations as they truthfully (τάληθές) exist by removing the falsehood (ψευδομένους) which prompted such ignorance (άνμαθία) (1, 2). His comments indicate a belief that speech has the power to recreate situations. It does not demonstrate an essence or truism but reveals through interpretation partial "knowledge" of real-world phenomena. Moreover, the power of speech extends beyond the discovery of existing conditions. Speech can also deceive the emotional and mental state of listeners by artificially stimulating sensory reactions through words; such action is, for Gorgias, the power of persuasion (πειθώ).

In addition to generating descriptive force, speech can dynamically evoke conditions or emotive responses in listeners which persuade and deceive the soul (6, 8). Persuasion can verbally evoke mental images which metaphorically recreate the feelings associated with fear- or joy-producing situations. Thus, the power of persuasion resides in its ability to conjure up and excite feelings and attitudes associated with past experiences. Such emotively descriptive reactions, Gorgias argued, are clearly observed in poetry and song, which are nothing more than words set to meter (9). For Gorgias, this is deception, since it is nothing more than words about experiences and not actual experiences. The ability to elicit emotive responses through symbols alone reinforces the notion of its inherent persuasive power (8; Freeman, *The Pre-Socratic Philosophers*, 363). The possibility for deception is apparent when words, which have no univocal meaning, are used within their context to guide the soul by interpreting and recreating an experience (11). Hence, a persuasive speaker could use the power of words to deceive listeners into becoming as frightened in the verbal re-creation of a battle as they would be if they actually were in the encounter. Gorgias argued that when "persuasion is conjoined (πρόσειμι) with speech it can mold the soul in any way it desires." Similar to medication, which can terminate either an illness or life itself depending on how it is used, so also can the power of speech be employed for either destructive or beneficial purposes (13, 14). In this respect, both Gorgias and Aristotle believed that the power of speech was itself amoral and depended upon the ethics of the user. The deception inherent in persuasion is not wrong in itself, nor does it necessarily evoke a false or misleading attitude.

The central point of Plato's criticism of Gorgias's rhetoric is that a true art avoids deception and concentrates on examining the nature of its subject. For Plato, that would be a rhetoric of the logos (*Gorgias* 501A-C; *Phaedrus* 262B). Gorgias, however, based his rhetorical theories upon philosophical premises which were far different from Plato's. Gorgias's position is best understood by examining the major tenets of communication which he proposed in his treatise entitled Περὶ τοῦ μὴ ὄντος ἢ Περὶ φύσεως (*On Non-Reality, or On Nature*). Olympiodorus indicates that Gorgias wrote the work in the eighty-fourth Olympiad or 444–441 B.C. (D-K 82. B2); a paraphrase of Gorgias's treatise was also made by [Aristotle] 979A–980B). Gorgias's primary tenets can be reduced to three divisions: "first, nothing actually exists; second, even if something actually did exist, it would be incomprehensible to man; third, even if comprehension could be attained, it could certainly not be articulated or explained" (65; Sextus Empiricus *adversus Mathematicos* 7. 65–87; D-K 82. B3). Such statements appear to be perplexingly illogical upon initial examination, but the fully developed elaboration of Gorgias's treatise, which certain scholars (e.g. Kennedy 1963, 14) have ignored, clarifies his position and theories of rhetoric.

The initial tenet of Gorgias's philosophy of communication is that "nothing actually exists" (οὐδὲν ἔστιν); that is, no one entity or concept can be idealized into existence (65; fragments cited in D-K 82. B3). We may be initially inclined to dismiss this notion as specious declamation, as indeed several scholars have done. Other writers, such as Isocrates (*Antidosis* 268–269; *Helen* 3–4), have taken Gorgias's statements literally, prompting a misinterpretation that Gorgias was little more than a nihilist (e.g. Dodds 6–8; Lesky 350; T. Gomperz, I, 392–396; Loenen 201–202; H. Gomperz 1–35). A careful examination of the fragments clearly reveals that Gorgias is not discussing existence of the physical world, which would be both an absurdity and a contradiction of the fundamental beliefs of his teachers and of his own empirical observations on sense-perceptions. Gorgias is using the verb "to be" (ἔστι) not as a linking verb but in an intransitive manner to indicate existence itself. Support for this interpretation is offered by Loenen (177–203; see also Kerford, 3–25), who considers τὶ ἔστι to be the basic thesis for all Eleatic thinkers. This concept is reinforced by noting his comments on other ontological concepts within the passage: "eternity" (ἀίδος); "endlessness" (ἄπειρος); and "creation" (ἀρχή) (68, 69). Gorgias so strongly opposed the belief in essences that he based subsequent arguments on the notion that concepts of the mind have no "real existence" at all (77–82). Platonic notions of ontological "essences" (for example, the ideal rhetoric) were absurdities to Gorgias. He viewed humans as functioning in an ever-changing world and manufacturing ideas that lose their "existence" the instant they pass from the mind of the thinker (68, 69). Accordingly, ideals attain existence only through the extrapolations of the mind and are dependent upon the referential perceptions of their creator (70). As such, they cannot exist without a manufactured antithesis or anti-model. By their very nature, they can form no ideal at all since each individual predicated ideals based on personal experiences. In this respect, each thinker's transient notion of the ideal rhetoric is an amorphous grouping of relative notions.

An understanding of Gorgias's initial tenets clarifies his second principle of communication: "that if anything actually did exist, it would be incomprehensible to man" (ὅτι εἰ καὶ ἔστιν, ἀκατάληπτον ἀνθρώπωι) (65). One of the crucial terms in this concept is "man," a term which standard translations often omit. For something to be comprehended it must be understood through the *human media* of understanding—sense-perceptions (77–78). Man's finite sense limitations, however, restrict him to perceptions based upon the optimum capacity of his senses. In this respect, thoughts beyond positivistic experience have no referential existence beyond the imaginative extrapolations of the thinker (79–82). Platonic notions of an idealized rhetoric were, for Gorgias, nothing more than myth, and they prompted him to maintain that even if they were to exist, their lack of physical referents, which are critical to human sense-perceptions, would make them incomprehensible to man (82). In short, total knowledge of any subject (including rhetoric) would be impossible and what would appear to be knowledge would be thoughts about observations that could only be partially understood through interpretations of our finite senses and cognitive preconceptions.

Gorgias's third and final tenet of communication directly relates to his theory of rhetoric: "that if anything were to be comprehended, it could not be articulated and communicated to others" (ὅτι εἰ καὶ καταληπτόν, ἀλλά τοί γε ἀνέξοιστον καὶ ἀνερμήνευτον τῶι πέλας) (65). For something to be actually understood, Gorgias argued, it must be experienced (83); Gorgias uses the term "τὰ ʽορατά," which means "physical entities." When communicated to others, however, sense-perceptions cannot provide an understanding of experience. Rather, speech (λόγος) conveys to others one's thoughts about a thing or an experienced idea (84). In this respect, speech can communicate references to experience, but as Gorgias argues, it "is not the same as that which the senses perceive and [which] actually exist" (84). Thus, even if it were possible to acquire an understanding of an ideal rhetoric, it could never be communicated to others, since it could have no referent to anything which could be perceived. Again, even if it could be perceived, man's finite sensory capacity could not recreate an idealized notion to others. Gorgias's adherence to such concepts of rhetoric compelled him to oppose the pursuit of an idealized rhetoric, since it could neither exist beyond individual speculation nor be understood or articulated to others. These principles of rhetoric aid in understanding Gorgias's concepts of antithesis and deception, which are evident in his extant orations.

Plato's plea for an ideal rhetoric was an attempt to create a formal, logical system of argumentation from universally affirmed and binding first principles or essences, causes and substances These first principles—"truisms"—would serve as starting points for reasoning about any particular situation with a view to discovering a proper course of action. Gorgias, on the other hand, rejected such ideals and developed an epistemology of rhetoric which allowed him to present a practical theory of resolving apparently incompatible choices by formulating arguments relevant to the specific circumstances of each unique situation (kairos). Plato desired a "logical" system into which any circumstance could be placed, but Gorgias developed a nonformal epistemology of rhetoric which allowed for the contingencies of interpretation and human nature that are inherent in any social circumstances, which inherently lack "ideal" or universally affirmed premises. Gorgias ascribed and contributed to a strong and recognized philosophical tradition which stressed probability, antithesis, relativism and sense-perception. As we shall see, Plato had no choice but to denounce Gorgias, for to acknowledge his philosophical position and his view of rhetoric would mean that Plato would have had to renounce the fundamental tenets of his own philosophy. Unfortunately, Plato's characterization of Gorgias presented both an unrepresentative account of an influential Greek thinker and a distorted interpretation of a major philosophy of rhetoric. The consequences are that the nature and spread of rhetoric's birth and its emergence through the Sicilian Sophistic have, to that extent, been misunderstood as well.

This inquiry into Gorgias's background and the extant fragments of his work provide insight into his role in the development of rhetorical theory and its subsequent spread from Sicily to the Hellenic world. Gorgias of Leontini was recognized as the father of sophists. If being the "father" of the sophists means stabilizing and standardizing the teaching of rhetoric as a discipline and serving as a model for sophists both from Sicily and throughout the Hellenic world, then such a title aptly fits Gorgias. Unlike most later sophists, however, he made no claim to teach virtue. He exercised a strong influence upon Tisias (and possibly even Corax), attained popularity, and attracted a number of students who became famous individuals. Indeed, Gorgias apparently attracted Isocrates away from Plato, as the conclusion of the *Phaedrus* implies. Gorgias thus became the teacher of the educator who is considered the founder of humanism (Jaeger 1990). Gorgias's concern with the pragmatics of human communication and its impact in daily, social interaction is certainly compatible with tenets of Isocrates' rhetoric. Gorgias's concern with education, particularly the relationship between how individuals think and express thoughts, placed him as an innovator of rhetoric within a continuum of discoveries on the human condition that marks this period of Greek thought. Gorgias was demonstrably popular and influential well beyond Leontini and Sicily. His impact spread popularity and enthusiasm for the First Sophistic throughout the Hellenic world and thus helped formalize rhetoric as a discipline. He also contributed to the evolution of the notion of paideia—that which constitutes intellectual excellence and validity. Gorgias was a pioneer but, in this respect, he was one of a series of pioneers developing new theories of knowledge.

Gorgias's main views on rhetoric reveal a strong philosophical position against Platonism. Gorgias's dialectical system of argument necessitated the advancement of contrary hypotheses which were contrived points of refutation. His methodology was based upon a system of investigation in which probable knowledge or opinion was synthesized from dichotomously antithetical positions. Gorgias saw no moral discrepancy in such a methodology of deception (in the sense previously defined) since it culminated in securing probable knowledge. He opposed Plato's views on a morally ideal rhetoric because Gorgias denied the existence of essences and consequently believed that whatever limited speculation man could advance toward such notions could only be absurd, incomplete, and irrelevant to pragmatic concerns. Man's finite limitations in securing information leading to knowledge restricted his ability to relativism and probability. Gorgias recognized that man's "knowledge" is both experiential and referential. Consequently, symbolic attempts to evoke persuasive consequences function only through the perceptions and notions of individual listeners.

The observations in this chapter were made to encourage a re-evaluation of Gorgias's epistemology of rhetoric. Plato's dialogues *Gorgias* and *Phaedrus* were blatantly unfair in their characterization of Gorgias and his contributions. Plato essentially criticized Gorgias for being "unphilosophical," that is, for being a pragmatically immoral opportunist who taught the appearance and not the reality of knowledge. Gorgias, however, would not recognize the basic tenets of Platonism (i.e., idealized ontologies); he was therefore considered to have no philosophy at all. Gorgias's own writings — as demonstrated here — reveal that he did indeed have a clear-cut epistemology and a genuine philosophy of rhetoric.

The "Art" of Sophistic Composition and the Flowering of Its Epistemology

Sophistic methods are markedly distinct from Aristotelian rhetoric. When Aristotle wrote his *Rhetoric*, well over a century after the beginning of the Sicilian Sophistic, he chose to view pistis (proof), and therefore process, as central to the revelation of krisis (judgment) and underscored enthymeme and example as the only rational methods for attaining judgment (1356b). Sicilian sophists, as we have seen, did not stress rational methods for attaining krisis but, rather, used nonrational, stylistic procedures for gaining the assent of listeners. The predominant techniques of rhetorical composition bear striking resemblance to techniques of poetic composition. Analytical structuring of dissoi logoi was a convention for coming to know, not rationally but stylistically (Havelock, 1982, 115–116; Untersteiner, 110, 120 (n. 86), 179; Cicero, *Brutus* 46, 47; Diodorus Siculus 12. 53. 4). Similarly, analogical thought in general, and metaphor in particular, is not realized through a rational process but, if effective, is apprehended immediately. Even Aristotle, whose *Rhetoric* is an effort to articulate a rational process for securing judgment, believed that metaphor could not be understood rationally (Aristotle, *Rhetoric* 1405a; *Poetics* 1459a). Since the early compositions of Homeric discourse, however, we have seen that conceptual structures were woven in and throughout stylistic structures, where loosely constructed or paratactic style dominated specifically directed hypotactic constructions. Highdefinitional hypotactic cues for the structuring of argument, which Chaim Perelman and L. Olbrechts-Tyteca called the mode "par excellence" (158) for argumentative composition, are subordinated to paratactic structuring where precise, rational cues are abandoned in place of dramatic, stylized periodic structures (Perry, 410–418 [esp. 412]; Havelock, 1982, 140; Kirk, 78–79). Attention was paid not to specific connecting terms associated with abstract thought, such as we would have with terms like "if," "then," "either," "or," and "therefore." Rather, earlier composers emphasized larger, formulaic patterns that emphasized a macroscopic pattern, such as the composition of an epic poem or an extended narrative of a heroic tale. Given this perspective, there is small wonder why the use of model speeches and compositions were so prevalent in sophistic technai (Aristotle, *Sophistici Elenchi* 183b–184a; Kennedy, 1959, 169–170).

The dominant concern for effect through style in sophistic rhetoric contrasted sharply with Aristotle's view of style and arrangement. For Aristotle, style (*lexis*) was essentially a "vulgar," but necessary, component to rhetorical discourse (*Rhetoric* 1403b, 1404a). "The whole substance of rhetoric," wrote Aristotle, "is directed toward opinion, but it is necessary that attention be given to it [style], not out of what is actually right, for rightly one should seek nothing more in a speech than to avoid pain or joy" (*Rhetoric* 1404a). Aristotle acknowledged style as the expression of emotion, but he saw it as an evil to be avoided; heightened aesthetic awareness had little place in Aristotle's techne of rhetoric. For Aristotle, style was "all for display and for the sake of the listener, for no one would teach geometry in such a manner," he claimed (*Rhetoric* 1404a). Yet it is precisely because rhetoric is not geometry—rather a public knowledge which is both realized and experienced—that its dimensions must be realized. Sophists composed rhetorical discourse on several levels. Meaning could be conveyed through antithetical and analogical thought indirectly while the cadence of the poetic discourse could be experienced to such an important degree that sophists could invent words as a "song without the chord and the lyre" (Aristotle, *Rhetoric* 1408a). Thus, in the same composition listeners could both appreciate the insights revealed in the arrangement and stylistic techniques while other listeners, who could not follow the "argument," could appreciate the cadence of co-existent but dissociated paratactic periods. In brief, connecting stylistic particles replace music with cadence, and *Kunstprosa* (prose-rhythm) provides a knowledge through sense awareness. It is for this reason that Aristotle may have acknowledged that there "is something of the kind" of rhapsodic and poetic composition in rhetoric (*Rhetoric* 1403b, 1404a). More accurately, as we have seen, rhapsodic and poetic composition are the essence of sophistic rhetoric.

The antithetical style characteristic of sophistic discourse is no less apparent in terms of arrangement. Where Aristotle's direct, rational discourse (*Rhetoric* 1410a-b) calls for thesis, sophistic rhetoric such as Gorgias's (e. g. *Epitaphios*; *Helen* 8; *Palamedes* 9, 22) calls for antithesis (D-K 82 [76]. B 6, 11, 11a). Where Aristotle called for rhetoric to state a thesis and prove it through systematic arrangement (τάξις), sophists disregarded precise, logical particles and used paratactic arrangement calling for a continuous, running style. Thus, style and arrangement, which receive only minimal attention in Aristotle's *Rhetoric*, are the grounds for invention in nonrational, indirect discourse which characterized much of pre-Aristotelian and later sophistic rhetoric. Thus, Aristotle used musical composition as an analogue to rhetorical discourse since both stress style and effect over rationalization leading to *krisis* (*Rhetoric* 1408a, 1414b).

Aristotle's opposition to sophistic rhetoric addressed the nature of rhetoric itself. Aristotle's *Metaphysics* shows that he distinguished between techne and episteme; he viewed the former as a system and the latter as a science (*Metaphysics* 1. 980a–981a; Reale, 18). For Aristotle, rhetoric is a techne since it is an activity — one does or makes rhetorical discourse. Physics, on the other hand, is a science or episteme — one attempts to understand (rather than "doing") nature. Giovanni Reale accounts for Aristotle's taxonomical distinctions by explaining that "art always has as its aim the production of a specific end," while the theoretical nature of science is purely speculative, "disinterested contemplation of the truth" (19; see also, Dodds [ed.], 1971, 27–28). According to Aristotle, sophists were preoccupied with emotion rather than "a productive settled disposition accompanied by reason" (Reale, 45, n. 9). The preference of sophists to use stylistic devices to create a synthesis of meaning indirectly — rather than to discover the pre-existing knowledge of first principles and the causes of things — would forever exclude sophistic thought from being epistemic. Lacking the rational approach necessary for a techne and the scientific rigor for an episteme, earlier rhetorics were outside Aristotle's conception of the discipline. For Aristotle, earlier "rhetorics" had no concern for proofs but only emotions and, as such, the very grounding of earlier technai "is removed from the subject" of his *Rhetoric* (1354a).

The accuracy of this view, of course, depends upon how one defines knowledge and the methods for acquiring it. Sophists such as Gorgias illustrate how heuristic techniques are grounded in stylistic devices and modes of arrangement. If (as was the case prior to Aristotle) style and arrangement are considered ways of coming-to-know, then they can be viewed as a generative force in composing not only discourse but thought. Thus, in contrast to Aristotle's views, a techne can have an epistemology if we accept the view that knowledge can be invented indirectly through "heuristics" of style and arrangement. As Empedocles illustrates, these presumptions were accepted by practitioners and thinkers of rhetoric before Aristotle. By Aristotle's notion of invention, however, Gorgias would be irrational and, therefore, not a serious thinker (*Rhetoric* 1404a, 1408b). Yet, by viewing style as a way of indirectly attaining judgment (krisis) not through proof (pistis) but through style (lexis) and arrangement (taxis), Gorgias can be viewed as composing eloquent discourse through a nonrational epistemology. In essence, sophistic discourse was driven by systems of pre- and nonrational ways of knowing — in practice long before Aristotle, although neither recognized nor accepted by him.

Aristotle's views on earlier rhetorics and rhetoricians have major implications for our study of the emergence of Hellenic rhetoric. As mentioned earlier, Aristotle would not regard sophistic "rhetoric" as a genuine techne but rather as a spurious illusion of a techne and hence no techne at all. His belief that real mastery of style was due to inspiration and not rationality only permitted a techne grounded in rationality as acceptable for the discipline of rhetoric. Given Aristotle's notion of rhetoric, style was little more than a necessary evil and arrangement a necessary constraint (*Rhetoric* 1408b, 1403b–1404a, 1414a-b, 1354a). Aristotle's rigid taxonomy separating techne from episteme, and style and arrangement from judgment and proof, categorically dismissed all prior treatments of rhetoric as fraudulent. Despite the opening statements of the *Rhetoric*, Aristotle's elitist rational standards for rhetoric closely approached his mentor, Plato. The firmness of their respective positions and the resulting influence of their thought made it appear that both Plato and Aristotle were not so much arguing against the Sicilian influenced sophistic rhetoric but rather that they were initiating the legitimate study of rhetoric as a serious discipline. Such a perspective was not only a disservice to the tradition of thought we have seen evolving but a misdirection that distorted rhetoric's history and devalued earlier intellectual, social and cultural contributions.

To offer an extended example of the variation in the two approaches, consider the construction of the information presented in this book. The author followed an Aristotelian, rational system of rhetorical composition. If the path blazed by Empedocles had been chosen, the composition would have balanced the rational against the nonrational, the certain against the probable, the emotions against the forces of reason. All of this would have been done in the poetic cadence of a sonorous hexameter verse, enlivened with analogies that flow forth from the springs of wisdom — an unreplenished font in which to dip the cup of inquiry and drink in the knowledge rippling forth from the source. As is obvious in the last few sentences, however, the author is no master of the sophistic style of argument. Yet, even being a student of Aristotelian composition with years of training in rational argument does not inhibit a recognition of the process and advantages of indirect, sophistic rhetoric and that it has an epistemology — which is more than either Plato or Aristotle would have cared to admit let alone openly acknowledge.

The perspectives presented here reveal that Aristotle's intolerance of sophistic rhetoric resulted in an imprecise portrayal of Empedocles and the sophists who followed him and tainted our views of the sophistic tradition which continued for centuries to rival Aristotelian rhetoric as a competing paradigm. The bias which dismissed sophistic methods deflected an awareness of the fundamental conceptual processes which structure all discourse. Such distinctions were unnecessary in Hellenic discourse when specialization was nonexistent. The fifth century B.C., which provided so many insights to knowledge, also produced a theory of rhetoric so constricted that later attempts to trace its development allocated commonly associated elements of rational discourse such as thought, conceptualization and expression to distinct disciplines (philosophy or rhetoric) rather than viewing a unified progression of cognitive processes.

Sicilian rhetoric emerged from the traditions of Homeric, rhapsodic, and logographic discourse to become a specialized logography. Grounded in pre-Socratic thought and poetic techniques, the sophists of Sicily created a system of expression that was effective for both civic and judicial functions. Integrating techniques of composition appropriate for both oral and written expression, they literally raised the level of public communication to an "art." In doing so, they presented powerful systems of expression that were superior to the individualistic methods of those who did not consider expression to be anything other than divine inspiration. Over the centuries, however, the notions of effective expression had evolved from the Homeric "gift" to a conscious, abstracted system. The effectiveness and power of Sicilian rhetoric in democratic communities could not be ignored by even adamant skeptics. The final view of rhetoric prior to Aristotle, then, is its impact in the most powerful of all Hellenic democracies: Athens.

Chapter V

The Platonic Rejection of Sophistic Rhetoric and Its Hellenic Reception

Socrates Questions Gorgias: The Rhetorical Vector of Plato's Philosophical Challenge

> But I neither was in agreement with these [philosophers] nor he who created and began the dispute with infinitely more seriousness and eloquence, Plato, whose *Gorgias* I read most carefully when I was in Athens with Charmadas; and what most surprised me about Plato in that work was that it seemed to me that as he was in the process of ridiculing rhetors he himself appeared to be the foremost rhetor."
> (Cicero, *De Oratore* 1. 11. 47)

Cicero's brief remark about Plato's *Gorgias*—uttered through *De Oratore*'s principle character Crassus—is ironic in two respects. First, Cicero's assertion that Plato was never a better rhetor than when ridiculing rhetoric reveals that Plato was "trapped" into the use of rhetoric as a way of arguing against it. Second, Plato was entrapped by technology. Despite his adamant opinion that direct oral dialogue was superior to writing, Plato was nonetheless relegated to the use of writing as a means of preserving both his ideas and those of his mentor, Socrates. The dialectic method of question-and-answer, provided the apparatus for such inquiry. That Plato is widely acknowledged as one of the great stylists of Antiquity (Levi 2) only makes the irony more acute. In both his techne and his technology, Plato was bound to the use of systems of articulating thought and expression—rhetoric and composition—that he found inferior. As a result of the use of rhetorical discourse and the technology of writing, we have the opportunity to explore Plato's *Gorgias*, a dialogue of unquestioned importance in understanding his view of sophistic rhetoric and the validity of his charges against it. Plato deals with the nature of rhetoric and the role of expression while he himself is engaged in those activities.

Plato Writes the Gorgias

Plato's dialogues are not the transcriptions of dialectic in action but rather are artistically composed discourse written to elicit a certain effect. In writing dialogues, Plato was using a technology of logography long associated with sophistic rhetoric. The first issue of *Philosophy and Rhetoric* contains Drew A. Hyland's "Why Plato Wrote Dialogues," a sympathetic defense of the reasons why Plato would stoop to script. Hyland's interpretation emphasizes how writing dialogues maintained the philosophical importance of the form of dialogue itself by not permitting readers to "forget to philosophize" (40) and that writing dialogues presents opposing viewpoints and thus preserves Plato's principle of not writing his "Platonic doctrine" (41). This argument will be disputed later in the chapter. The importance of Hyland's position is that it explains Plato's dialogues as acts of philosophy; that is, Hyland's presumption is that what Plato is doing is philosophizing. Yet, the question-and-answer format of Platonic dialogues also reveals their rhetorical vector. In the *Gorgias*, the presentation is better understood as rhetorical argument of the kind associated with sophistic rhetoric.

According to Dodds, the *Gorgias* is "now universally accepted" (18) as belonging to the first of the three major groupings of Plato's dialogues, called the "early," "Socratic" or "aporetic" dialogues. The classification of the *Gorgias* in this first group is important, since one of the salient features of the early dialogues is that "Socrates asks questions" (Meyer [1980] 282), a feature not characteristic in later dialogues. For Socrates, the *Gorgias* is an effort to arrive at an answer to the worth of sophistic rhetoric as a contributor to knowledge. To engage in this activity, Socrates questions the movement's most prestigious representative, Gorgias of Leontini. As we have seen, however, for both the actual Gorgias and Plato's dialogue-character, the ends and process of sophistic discourse are in marked contrast to Plato, and here, Socrates' position. For Gorgias, rhetoric is the process of justifying answers or propositions to and by a public audience. From the sophistic perspective, as Meyer emphasizes, "questioning serves only as a pretext for giving his own opinion as an answer" ([1980] 281) and thus has a far different purpose (282) in the Socratic debate than the (early) Platonic process for arriving at Truth. By appearance and intent, then, the Platonic and sophistic methods of dealing with questions would seem to be at odds. Plato's dialogue, however, not only uses the dialectical method of question-and-answer as a heuristic for advancing propositions by Socrates, but the *Gorgias* itself — composed as one extended argument — more resembles sophistic argumentation than the method and form in which it appears might lead one to think.

Remembering that the *Gorgias* is a fictive, literary composition helps to reestablish the nature and parameters of Plato's treatise. As the first great thinker to solidify a philosophy based on abstraction (Havelock 1963/1982, 286; Sesonske 78), it is not surprising that Plato would have control of his language. Nor is it particularly surprising that he would (reluctantly) resort to a sophistic technology that would artificially simulate the dynamics of the dialectical process. What is extraordinary, but not immediately apparent, is that this shift from oral deliberation to writing would do much more than simply record verbal interactions. The change in medium so transformed the process that the interactions were now dialogues in form only and dialectic only in appearance. In effect, as noted by Skousgaard, "the Platonic Dialogues instantiate in literary form the dialogical-ritual of Socrates much the same as the genre of tragic poetry instantiates the ritual of value-reconstruction" (376).

Recognizing Platonic dialogues as literary creations is central to assessing his criticism of sophistic rhetoric. "It is a constantly recurring characteristic of Platonic dialogues," notes Friedlander ([1958] 155), "that Socrates contrasts the kind of conversation he conducts with the lectures of the Sophists." Plato's "writing" of dialectic events — as opposed to the spontaneous deliberations of several participants — introduces a dimension of mediation not only in the level of writing but in the interpretive function of the author.

In the *Meno*, for example, Socrates explicitly discusses Gorgias's habit of answering questions in an elaborate and detailed manner (70B), a trait characteristic of sophists. In the *Gorgias*, however, Plato has his Socrates chide Gorgias for long-winded answers (449C) and directs him to limit his responses to short, direct replies. Socrates' insistence on dialogic conversation rather than rhetorical elaboration is not unique to the *Gorgias*. In the *Protagoras* (329A), Socrates rebukes sophists and politicians who respond to questions as if they were reciting passages from written books, which can neither answer nor ask but give only the same long response. Socrates even rebukes Gorgias, as Quimby illustrates, for having "taught Polus to make speeches but not to answer questions" (76). In the *Gorgias* (453C), Socrates asserts that it is by asking Gorgias questions—rather than merely stating his own view—that progress in argument can be made. Surprisingly, Gorgias, the master of rhetorical embellishment and the elaboration of a thesis (449B; 458B,C), agrees. Plato has modified the characteristic dialogue pattern of the real Gorgias and composed the dialogue character in a manner that permits him only to respond to questions in a dialectical rather than rhetorical manner. In effect, as Friedlander comments, "Chairephon, whom Socrates is using as a kind of advance guard against the enemy, knows as much about the Socratic art of asking questions as Polus, the pupil of Gorgias, knows about the art of his master" (93).

What takes place in the dialogue is ostensibly an argument over two competing views of knowing but agreement on the method of deliberation—that is, Gorgias's concession to debate in the dialectical mode. It is difficult to imagine that the real Gorgias, noted for his elegant prose, would have agreed to such a format. It is also ironic to note that as the dialogue develops it is Socrates who elaborates his statements in detail and Gorgias is reduced to virtually passive silence. Plato abandons the crisp, direct question-and-answer format promised at the introduction of the dialogue (462A) when an extended statement benefits Socrates's position, an inconsistency which Kauffman calls "an unpardonable blunder" (121). Regardless of how the actual Gorgias may have reacted to Socrates' command for short answers, it is obvious that Plato's literary control has done more than "controlled the opposition of character" (Levi 17). When Plato takes license by rewriting the characters, he can no longer claim a representation of the mode and form of the dialectic. In altering the nature and essence of his characters, he has transformed dialectic from a philosophical to a rhetorical activity. The act of writing a dialectic, as opposed to participating in or recording one, transformed Platonic dialogues into rhetorical compositions. In sum, Plato's criticism of sophistic deliberation centers on his distaste for long-winded propositional arguments rather than dialectical interaction. Yet, his *Gorgias* is itself one detailed argument of proposition under the guise of a dialogue.

The Constituents of the Dialectical Situation and Its Rhetorical Function

To say that Plato engaged in rhetorical discourse when he wrote such dialogues as the *Gorgias* is to echo a commonplace uttered as long ago as the quotation from Cicero at the beginning of this chapter. Yet, asserting that Plato's dialogues are rhetorical arguments does not help us to understand the nature of his literary enterprise unless the nature of these "rhetorical arguments" is specified. Plato's compositions are cast as dialectical arguments: immediate, live, correlative, rigorous and interactive (Kaufer 64, n.4). Dialectic is an inventional situation, with cooperative inter-locutors seeking to approach a *telos*, an immutable end, whose validity is not measured by the judgments of participants or the audience present but by a universal standard. "One of the basic accusations against writing," argues Lentz, "was that the written word could not reply to questions, and therefore could not explain the intended meaning of its words" (15). Plato's simulated dialogues attempt to capture the oral features of a spontaneous dialectic. The positioning of questions, the framing of responses are all cast in a manner that recreates the best features of the Socratic method of probing for Truth. However, actual spontaneous interaction is momentary — thus lost to all but those within hearing range. Plato's desire to extend his audience beyond those physically present left him no choice but to freeze the moment through writing — in a sense, to abstract a pragmatic event by stabilizing it through simulation. In doing so, however, Plato introduced a new dimension to his simulated dialectic — he fictionalized the possibility of responses of his interlocutors. In dramatizing philosophy, Plato engaged in the choice and selection of responses. These two dimensions — writing and re-creation — shifted the nature and function of dialectic from a non-fictive to a mimetic event and introduced a rhetorical vector to the simulated dialogues. In short, the *Gorgias* is dialogue only in appearance and dialectic only in form.

One of the most important elements in Plato's *Gorgias* is the characterization of participants. While Rendall accurately calls Plato's *Gorgias* an act of fictive utterances (176), he also asserts that statements in the *Gorgias* do "represent the natural utterances of characters who speak in them" (176). Interlocutors participating in the dialogue on the nature of rhetoric and the requirements for a legitimate techne in effect stand in both for representative ways of thinking and for the prevailing social standards of evaluating thought. Gorgias and his apprentice Polus, for example, respectively constitute both the foundation of sophistic thought (Friedlander 92) and its future form. Characterized as the founder of sophistic rhetoric, the elderly Gorgias represents the most mature and refined personification of their movement; Polus is the promising student of that tradition (466 B,C). Gorgias and Polus represent a contrast to Socrates and his apprentice, Chairephon. Together these two pairs represent the maturation of both clearly distinct views and the consequences of their enactment through disciples. Callicles, the final character in the dialogue, has little to contribute to the understanding of the nature of rhetoric. Rather, he embodies the society that will either benefit or suffer from the practice of rhetoric. Grounded in expediency and valuing matters only in terms of their social consequences, Callicles represents a segment of the Athenian community whose democratic tendencies elevated public approbation as the measure of validity to a degree that — in Plato's mind — put at risk the fundamental ideals of virtue (arete) and intellectual excellence (paideia). Callicles and his colleagues are the audience which will ultimately enact the consequences of the rhetoric chosen through deliberation. Callicles' participation and questions express the popular sentiment (481C,D) of the Athenian society that he represents and gives the Athenian community its voice in the dynamics of the dialectical deliberation.

Plato's composition of dialogue characters does more than center the locus of conversational control with the author; it reveals an argumentative technique that is established in oral discourse but modified in literary composition. Since its inception with Zeno, the process of question-and-answer was inherent in the dialectical method. This process, a common practice in oral deliberations, served many functions. It helped interlocutors position the *stasis* (point of conflict) of deliberation by establishing agreement on key terms. It served both to reaffirm norms and to regulate untenable assertions. All such functions were based on the presumption that independent minds were at work contributing to a common goal — the most sensitive understanding of the topic under examination — and that a reality of that understanding existed independent of the individuals present. The task of participants, then, was to pool intellectual resources in a united effort to reach that understanding. The audience, in turn, represents not an *ad hoc* collection of listeners, but rather a group of listeners who constitute a "normal" group of reasonable individuals who offer the possibility of being swayed by reasonable arguments.

Based on such presumptions, the method of question-and-answer became both an inventive and corrective device for reaching a goal. As Welch notes, "Plato praised philosophical rhetoric because it depends on the active use of dialectic. . . . Without dialectic, there is no real rhetoric for Plato" (10). Plato's *writing* of a dialogue, however, altered the nature of dialectical deliberations to the extent that it (ironically) gave only the outward appearance of the deliberative process. The interaction of independently thinking minds was replaced by the isolated thoughts of one writer: Plato. Presumptions of deliberations were regulated in question-and-answer form only within the mind of Plato and not by independent thinking of participants. In short, rather than having the recording of an actual dialogue that captures a dialectic, the *Gorgias* is a monologic composition in dialogic form. That is, the composed interactions are mimetic and directive rather than non-fictive and spontaneous. Distinctions between its apparent form and its actual composition expose processes in the composing of the *Gorgias* that better explain its nature and its eventual implications.

Plato Composes Reality

While the entire *Gorgias* is composed in dialogue format, the opening passages are particularly important for understanding the argumentative vector of Plato's question-and-answer scheme. Socrates' early questions are an effort to gain consensus on critical notions. Concepts such as techne and *dunamis* (capacity) are treated early in the discussion (e.g. 451A, 452E) and are used as the basis for weighing the meaning of the more essential notions of *dike* (justice), *arete* (excellence), *paideia* (intellectual excellence) and ultimately rhetoric itself. In short, the early questions of Socrates are directed toward establishing a consensus on the nature of such terms as "art," "system" and "capacity." This process was a necessary prelude to revealing sophistic rhetoric's nature and evaluating its credibility for goals of justice, excellence and educational ideals.

Plato uses Socrates' early questions to illustrate that consensus about the meaning of terms such as techne and dunamis not only form a starting point of agreement but that agreement constitutes the "reality" of such terms. Plato's question-and-answer technique presupposes the existence of such concepts and the interlocutors' desire to discover their meaning. This starting point—that such concepts have independent existence—is the foundation for Plato's subsequent arguments. That is, the recognition of the reality of such notions forms the basis for evaluating items under discussion. "Ontology," as Perelman indicates, "would thus serve as the basis for a hierarchy of forms of conduct" (103). Agreement in the form of favorable answers to Socrates' questions constitutes tacit recognition of the ontological existence of such terms. Once agreed upon by Gorgias and Polus, Socrates has the ontological foundation, the starting point of argument, to then evaluate sophistic rhetoric. In actuality, however, the starting point of the *Gorgias* is a *petitio principii*—a technique of question-begging. The ontological existence of critical notions is presumed not verified. Moreover, such presumptions are ones which actual sophists—not the characters created by Plato—would likely have contested. The fragments of Gorgias's own works, for example, clearly reveal that he would have contested Plato's assumptions of reality. The actual Gorgias would have redirected the argument to determine if meaning is independent of human interaction and social consensus rather than acquiescing to Socrates's opening questions.

Plato has not revealed Reality; he has composed one for his readers. Through both direct and indirect interrogative sentences, Plato has so composed the interaction of the participants that the starting points—the existence of an essential nature of rhetoric subject to examination—are presumed rather than deliberated. The framework of the questions presupposes both the existence of rhetoric's "truthful" reality (517A) and the methodology for seeking an understanding of it. The ostensible question-and-answer scheme is really a heuristic for establishing a shared view of reality. The opening passages of the *Gorgias* offer a convenient format to choose and select those features that Plato believes constitute the legitimacy of a discipline. Plato's opposition to the view that public consensus constitutes a standard of judgment (502E) is based on the presumption that such decisions are based not on the validity of a point but rather communal opinion. Plato's own view, however, is predicated on his opinions that justice exists independent of agreement and that abstraction toward an idea(l) (508C) is the standard for determining validity. Lost within Plato's presumptions is the fact that sophists who practiced rhetoric did use abstraction but did not presuppose that it would lead to essences independent of human cognition, articulation and social validation. The process used in the *Gorgias* is similar to its function in the *Phaedrus*, which Murray describes "as the erection of a structure (albeit rhetorical) which *requires as its foundation* the dialectical process" (281). In short, Plato's use of questioning is a heuristic employed not to discover Truth but rather to create his interpretation of reality in the minds of readers.

Excluding the current practices of legal argument and the Socratic method of teaching, contemporary procedures for arriving at knowledge utilize propositions rather than questions. The trend, as Meyer (1988 4) reveals, is that "answers have become propositions, questions have disappeared as sophistic or eristic, at any rate as the opposite of knowledge." In what is perhaps the ultimate irony for the Platonic method, the long-sustained, thesis-driven propositions characteristic of sophistic rhetoric have become more representative of the mode of articulating understanding and opinion than the form of question-and-answer. Yet, Plato's method for understanding had a tremendous impact on philosophy and on the history of rhetoric. "Actually," observed Stewart, "Plato's purpose, his method, and rhetoric's adaptability are difficult to separate. General scholarly opinion seems to be that Plato was never in doubt about what the function of rhetoric should be, but the method had to be developed" (120). Stewart's point bears directly on the topic of this chapter, which has sought to identify the method Plato actually employed in the *Gorgias*. More specifically, "Plato cannot," as Welch accurately argues, "divide the activity of dialectic from rhetoric" (17). This chapter supports Stewart's pervasive observation and particularly Welch's view of the "interaction of dialectic and rhetoric" (18): we cannot divide the activity of rhetoric *from* Plato's dialectic. Plato's *Gorgias* employed question-and-answer as a rhetorical heuristic. Socrates' opening questions are based on the supposition that real natures driving critical concepts are waiting to be discovered—as opposed to the sophistic view that meaning is an act of abstraction through social consensus.

Henry W. Johnstone, Jr. has spent much of his scholarly career demonstrating "that the distinction between finding the truth in philosophy and finding the proper rhetorical devices for propagating it cannot be maintained" (74). There is little doubt that Plato considered dialectic the appropriate device for philosophy but did not realize or acknowledge that when he had his characters answer and respond he was propagating "truth" through a rhetorical device: the heuristic of question-and-answer. Plato's question-and-answer form is itself a heuristic of argument: the choice and selection of data and method based on preference in the form of an independently logical ideal. That position, as richly and thoroughly realized by current scholarship, is precisely the point of contention between Plato and the real Gorgias. In an actual dialogue between the two men, there would have been no agreement to the opening questions and, therefore, no subsequent arguments developed from a shared starting point. When Plato composed his dialogue, he ought to have structured his question-and-answer scheme to argue for a shared view of reality rather than to presuppose it; that is, Plato could have had the dialogue character Socrates engage Gorgias and Polus in questions that would have sought to establish a shared basis of agreement that ontology was indeed the reality and the standard for the evaluation of sophistic rhetoric. Plato could not compose a true simulation of a dialogue which sought to establish a shared basis of agreement since the validation of an ontological reality would then rest with the interlocutors' agreement and not its independent existence. Plato's belief in the independent existence of ideas would restrict him from having Socrates argue for a shared view of reality, since human agreement should not be the test of its validity.

From this perspective it is clear that Plato's composition of question-and-answer differs radically from the transcription of a dialectical conversation. Rather, it is more accurately characterized as argument: an inventional tool to advance a position and secure the auditor's agreement — in short, a rhetorical device. The "long-winded" statements by Socrates that occur toward the close of the dialogue constitute propositional statements about the nature of rhetoric as practiced by the sophists. These propositional declarations are based on the agreement of critical terms reached (enforced) earlier. In this sense, Plato's initial use of question-and-answer in the *Gorgias* evolved into an argument that would eventually be composed in a propositional mode. Because this heuristic presupposes a view of reality, and is initiated from Plato's desire to think of things in such a manner, it is best understood as rhetorical in nature and dialectical in appearance. The argument of the *Gorgias*, initiated from a starting point that only the sophists Plato composed as characters would likely have agreed with, illustrates the rhetorical vector of Plato's dialectical method but offers an explanation of why, as cited in the opening passages of this chapter, Cicero saw Plato as a rhetor at his best when he was arguing against rhetoric in the *Gorgias*.

While Plato's dialogues have been respected by intellectuals for centuries, the immediate Athenian audience represented by Callicles in the dialogue, made a far different judgment. The sophistic rhetoric exemplified by Gorgias became immensely popular. On that basis, Plato's rejection of sophistic rhetoric failed. Athenians continued to study and to apply the techniques of Sicilian-based rhetoric. While Plato's views may well have gained philosophical respect, pragmatic systems of rhetoric thrived in Athens and throughout the Hellenic world. Sophistic rhetoric prompted other individuals such as Antiphon and Isocrates to develop techniques and educational programs that also rivaled Plato's views. Eternally successful as a philosopher, Plato's compositions failed to convince his immediate audience of the shortcomings of sophistic rhetoric.

Forensic Rhetoric:
Antiphon's *On the Murder of Herodes*

The Attic orator Antiphon had such an impact on the emerging discipline of rhetoric that some ancient writers thought of him as its founder, although Corax and Tisias were likely already practicing the art of rhetoric shortly after the time of Antiphon's birth in 480 B.C. (Philostratus 498; [Plutarch] *Vitae decem oratorum* 832 c, d). Antiphon's techniques of forensic argument were so advanced that his contemporaries considered him "too clever" in legal matters and even lampooned his ability in public plays (Philostratus 499; Thucydides 8. 68). To Thucydides, however, Antiphon was "a man in no way inferior to any of his fellow Athenians in moral character and . . . was the most competent man to give advice to any who sought his expertise in advocacy in judicial and public matters" (8. 68). Thucydides was not alone in his praise of Antiphon as the premier forensic rhetorician of his day, for even Socrates, who had few positive comments on rhetoric, did regard Antiphon positively as a teacher of the oratorical art (*Menexenus* 236a).

Centuries later, Antiphon continues to maintain a prominent position in the history of rhetoric for essentially two reasons. He was the first Athenian logographer, and he wrote one of the earliest rhetorical manuals ([Plutarch] *Vitae decem oratorum* 832 c,d; Antiphon *Fragmenta* C3). In addition to these accomplishments, he developed and popularized notions of argument and advocacy which were compatible with systems developed in the Sicilian Sophistic and which persisted throughout the history of rhetoric. The interest in rhetoric at Athens not only fostered an intellectual climate for Attic orators such as Antiphon but also attracted non-Athenian intellectuals (*metoekoi*), who promoted discourse as an emerging discipline worthy of serious study. The range of perspectives exhibited by these foreign sophists, from the poetic embellishment of Gorgias to the agnostic relativism of Protagoras, prompted experimentation in the study of discourse unbridled by conventional rules and helped Antiphon develop effective rhetorical techniques in judicial argumentation. In fact, Antiphon's concepts of "probable cause," "motive," "intent," and "presumption" in litigation represent one of the earliest applications of such techniques, predating Aristotle by several decades.

The significance of Antiphon's works is also acknowledged by modern scholars such as Richard C. Jebb, who claims that "Antiphon stands first among the orators of the Attic canon" (vol. 1, 18). Although Antiphon's seminal influence is well-recognized by both ancient and contemporary writers, little research has been done to synthesize his contributions (Jebb vol. 1, 18–19; Dobson 21). Consequently, studying Antiphon's notions of discourse — particularly as revealed through his discourse — provides valuable insight into the rhetoric of Hellenic litigation.

According to [Plutarch], one of Antiphon's most admired orations was *On the Murder of Herodes*, an oration written by Antiphon but, as was customary in Hellenic advocacy, presented by the defendant himself ([Plutarch] *Vitae decem oratorum* 833d). Jebb believes that this plea was the most important of the speeches which Antiphon wrote for actual delivery (Jebb vol. 1, 55). Unfortunately, *On the Murder of Herodes* has been scantily analyzed. Excluding scattered comments on style, Jebb limits his treatment to cursory descriptive remarks (vol. 1 55–62). John F. Dobson's approach is similar to Jebb's, except that even less emphasis is put on analysis (34–43). Kathleen Freeman (1963) and K. J. Maidment (1968) both present readable translations of the oration but provide no substantive analysis. Lastly, George Kennedy clearly acknowledges the contributions of Antiphon throughout *The Art of Persuasion in Greece*, but he limits observations to one sentence: "The fifth speech, *On the Murder of Herodes*, is apparently the latest of the three [orations actually delivered in court] and is somewhat better in all these respects than the other two, though still without complete self-assurance and polish" (132). Thus, the most popular and influential works on the subject shed little light on Antiphon's notions of argument and advocacy in this important case.

According to K. J. Dover, the actual case was tried c. 414/413 B.C. (55). The unnamed defendant and Herodes were both passengers on a ship bound for Aenus. In the course of the voyage, a storm arose and the ship was forced to dock at Methymna on the northwest coast of Lesbos. Since the ship on which the accused and Herodes were passengers had no covered deck, they were transferred to an enclosed ship. The men drank excessively on board this second ship. At some point, Herodes, apparently by consent, left but was never seen again. An exhaustive search revealed no trace of him, and eventually the accused left Mytilene charged with murder. The prosecution claimed that the defendant went on shore, killed Herodes with a stone and threw the body into the sea from yet another ship. As evidence, the prosecution offered the testimony, prompted by torture, of both a slave and a foreigner—as well as a note in which the accused explicitly stated that he had killed Herodes. To combat this prosecution, Antiphon concentrated his defense on four issues: (1) the trial, as it was conducted, was illegal; (2) the testimony of the tortured witnesses was unreliable; (3) the alleged note confirming the murder was spurious; and (4) favorable religious signs indicated the innocence of the accused. This structuring of discourse provides information of theoretical importance in determining the nature of Antiphon's advocacy and prompts an examination of the issues as a means of revealing argumentative strategies.

Understanding Antiphon's initial argument about the legality of the trial requires a summary of the legal procedure for homicide cases. According to Aristotle's *Athenian Constitution*, Solon retained the laws and procedures for homicide cases established by Draco (7.1). Under normal conditions, a charge of murder would have been tried before the Areopagus (the Athenian High Court) with each side speaking; death was the possible penalty for conviction (*Athenian Constitution* 57.3). The oration establishes that the defendant in this case, however, was not prosecuted on an indictment of murder but as a "wrongdoer," which usually had the connotation of "thief" rather than "murderer" (9). Phrasing the charge in such a way served to remove the trial from the Areopagus and place it in the Dikastery of the Eleven (*Athenian Constitution* 52.1). The argument for the defense was that the charge of wrongdoing was directed toward common criminals. Since the accused was charged with murder, he ought not to be subject to the dictates of a court which did not normally deal with this crime. The higher court of the Areopagus offered the defense two benefits which were not provided in the Dikastery. In a trial before the Areopagus, the defendant would have the legal right of voluntary exile (13, 87) and the prosecution would have to take the traditional religious oath (11, 96). Antiphon believed the oath would deter the prosecution from presenting false information (95). Freeing the prosecution and witnesses from the religious oath gave the opposition such liberty that Antiphon claimed, "you have invented laws for yourself" (12). The religious grounding for oaths and testimony was a critical element in Antiphon's advocacy. Antiphon wisely avoided alienating the listeners who would decide the case by stressing that the dispute was not about their credibility but was an attempt to avoid the possibility of an unjust retrial. In fact, Antiphon explicitly told the judges that "even if you were not bound by oath or law, I would still entrust my life to [your] vote" (8).

Antiphon's counterplea of jurisdiction, one of the earliest uses of such a concept, was presented to shift the burden of illegality from the court to the prosecution by arguing that the prosecution had an unfair advantage in being able to participate in this proceeding as well as any subsequent one in the Areopagus (8–19). Antiphon supported this charge of judicial illegality with three points. First, the malefaction charge provided the prosecution with two opportunities to secure a favorable decision. If acquitted of the charge, the prosecutor could claim that the unspecified wrongdoing was for a reason other than murder and re-prosecute with a charge of murder. Conversely, if the prosecution won the case, they could claim the malefaction charge as murder and demand the life of the accused. "And yet," argued Antiphon, "how could anything more terrible be contrived; if you and your colleagues persuade this court once your goal is attained, but if I should be acquitted once, I would [still] have the same [threat] remaining" (16).

Antiphon argued that all these injustices culminated when the defendant was denied the right to post the three sureties bail and was thus severely impeded in preparing for the case. Thus, Antiphon attempted to gain the sympathy of his listeners by stressing his alleged lack of preparation (1–7). Moreover, Jebb writes that the harsh and illegal treatment of the accused may have been partly the result of ill will between the Mytilenians and the Athenians, compounded by "the fact that Herodes had been an Athenian citizen" (vol. 1, 58). Jebb's view is entirely plausible, for the case was held only two years before Lesbos openly revolted from Athens in 412 B.C. and the tension existing between the two states would account for the emotional opening of the oration. Technically, however, Antiphon's plea of the trial's illegality was groundless. As Maidment correctly indicates, an alien from a state such as Lesbos could be brought before a Heliatic court and tried as a "wrongdoer" even if the crime were murder (152). Such pleas, whether technically correct or not, reveal a conscious effort to establish a foundation for subsequent arguments. Antiphon attempted to clarify the nature of the situation and the appropriate parameters of argument in order to structure the thoughts of the listeners to favor the defendant.

After exploring the legality of the case, Antiphon concentrated on a brief narration of the events. He sought to establish that neither a motive nor an opportunity for the accused to commit the crime ever existed. An interesting characteristic of Antiphon's analysis is his specific references to the notion of "probability" (e. g. 26, 27, 37, 43, 45, 63), the attribute of Sicilian rhetoric which we have seen as the foundation of the precepts of Corax, Tisias, and Gorgias. This narration, which followed an emotional opening, may be interpreted as establishing a set of presumptions from which arguments based on probability could be advanced to counter the prosecution's charges. Antiphon intended to destroy any notion of causality which could lead to a probable motive for homicide.

Antiphon demonstrated a sophisticated use of rational construction of probable intent through the establishment of a pyramid of inferences—a revolutionary departure from the predominantly emotive pleas which characterized the oratory of earlier generations. First, Antiphon argued that Herodes and the accused were on separate, unrelated business. Next, he restated the prosecution's claim that Herodes was killed on shore after having left the second ship. Antiphon rationalized that the accused, whom witnesses had confirmed as not having left the second ship, could not have been involved. His third point was that if Herodes had been allegedly hit with a stone and thrown overboard from a third ship, that ship could have been brought from the harbor only by a man who either left the ship Herodes was originally on or who was never on board. Furthermore, the stone and third ship used in the alleged murder were never discovered. Lastly, Antiphon stressed how the prosecution argued that "when they discovered the blood [stains on the second ship] they said [Herodes] had died" (29), but abandoned the argument when the blood was discovered to have come from sacrificed animals (29). Antiphon's argumentative form of establishing probability anticipates what Cicero would later term *enumeratio*, or "a method in which one remaining point is unavoidably confirmed after many other points have been explained and invalidated" (*De Inventione* 1. 45). This method was specifically used to discount the probability that the accused had any motive for the alleged homicide (the oration, as was customary, is presented by the defendant himself):

> What indeed was my intent in killing this man, for there was no hatred at all between me and him. The [prosecution] ventures to say that I killed this man as a favor, but who has ever performed [such an act] to gratify another? No one, I believe. Certainly great hatred [must] arise for [murder] to be committed, and the development of such a plot is grossly evident, but there was no hatred whatsoever between me and him. . . . I tell you these things to show that I had no motive to murder the man (57–60).

Even though Antiphon heavily emphasized probability to establish points, he never, as Jebb indicates, bothered to establish any confirming alibi (vol. 1, 61), other than the claim of witnesses who would verify that the accused never left the second ship. Such an omission, however, should not lessen the importance of Antiphon's attempt to introduce the notions of "intent" or "motive" as a grounding for probable actions. Although Antiphon may appear content to reduce motives and opportunities to improbability, the implication is that the lack of probability of a motive or opportunity itself serves as an implicit alibi. In fact, Antiphon's development of the concept of "presumption," which he employs in this oration (e.g. 83) and discusses theoretically in the extant fragments of his rhetorical manual (*Fragmenta* C3), would account for his reliance upon motive and probability as sufficient to make the articulation of an alibi unnecessary. It is also important to note that every major point argued from probability and presumption was confirmed by witnesses so that the inferences would be warranted (20, 22, 24, 28, 30, 35, 56, [possibly 61], 83).

Antiphon extended his case beyond inductive inquiry, however, and often concentrated on invalidating the testimony of the two witnesses for the prosecution, one a slave and the other a freeman (3052). The freeman, who was tortured by the prosecution immediately after the alleged murder, actually offered no incriminating evidence against the accused (30). It is also likely that this freeman was non-Athenian since, by law, no Athenian citizen could be tortured (Bonner 74). The slave, tortured days after the event, contradicted the testimony of the first witness by naming the defendant as the guilty party (31). Consequently, Antiphon was compelled to examine the credibility of this incompatible evidence in a manner which would lend the most weight to his defense. Centering his attack on the examination of the tortured slave, Antiphon asserted that "without question, the slave was probably pledged his freedom" in return for testimony favorable to the prosecution "(31). This promise of freedom, coupled with relief from torture, provided ample likelihood that the slave would falsify his testimony. Aristotle clarifies Antiphon's reasoning in the *Rhetoric* by explaining that certain men under such conditions "will be forced by torture to utter false claims rather than the truth, and even to endure to the end rather than speak the truth, and others ready to invent lies so as to more quickly end [the ordeal]" (1377a; Cope 1867, 200–201). The dubious nature of such "proof" was emphasized by Antiphon's claim that later, when the slave "knew he was going to die, he immediately proclaimed the truth and said that these men had persuaded him to lie about me [i.e., the defendant]" (33). Antiphon's comment is also consistent with Aristotle's belief in the natural superiority of, and the inclination for, truth (*Rhetoric* 1355a). In fact, Antiphon's use of the word "proclaimed" (ἐχρῆπω from χράω) to indicate the slave's revelation of truth has religious connotations and is frequently taken to indicate a divinely inspired response. The presumption of the intrinsic force of truth in Hellenic discourse is important to note in Antiphon's argument, for it stands in marked contrast to the relativistic perspective of sophists such as Protagoras or Gorgias.

Perhaps the entire question of consistency could have been clarified if a cross-examination of the slave had been possible, particularly since, as Bonner affirms, cross-examination of a slave-witness with torture was permissible (70). Antiphon, however, indicates that the prosecution illegally put the slave to death before a cross-examination was possible (46). Antiphon's treatment of this entire use of slave-testimony exemplifies a rhetorical characteristic which George Kennedy criticizes: "He [Antiphon] tends to pick out one argument and present it early in the speech, and he does not systematically exhaust all possible arguments" (1963, 131). Antiphon never effectively treated the testimony of the first witness, the tortured foreigner, and never mentioned whether his own witnesses, which he called on so often throughout the trial, were treated in the same manner which he so bitterly denounced. These gaps in the defense, coupled with the already noticeable omission of an alibi, reveal serious weaknesses in Antiphon's case.

Denied the opportunity to cross-examine the slave, Antiphon attacked the authenticity of a note submitted by the prosecution, which was presented as evidence linking the accused with the murder of Herodes. According to the defense, the prosecution discovered a note on board the ship stating "that I had killed the man" (53). The prosecution argued that this note was sent by the accused through his slave-accomplice to a man named Lycinus (53–56). Antiphon's sole method of refuting this charge was again to argue from probability. The defense asserted that there was no need for a messenger if the slave himself was an accomplice and able to convey the simple message verbally. Antiphon's rationale is plausible, even assuming that the slave was literate. Yet, Antiphon shifted from demonstrating the lack of need for such a note to discussing inconsistencies with the testimony of the slave who "said, when tortured, that he himself had killed him [Herodes]" (54). Antiphon exposed the contradiction of such opposing views by reminding his listeners of the earlier claim that "the slave confessed under torture that he had helped me kill him [i.e., the defendant]" (§39).

Antiphon argued that the opposition's case rested upon inconsistent and incompatible claims: the defendant had a slave as an accomplice and the slave committed the murder alone. If the first statement by the slave was correct, then the "unnecessary" note would have further linked the slave and the defendant as accomplices and destroyed Antiphon's argument, which was designed to invalidate the note and any possible association with an act of murder. If, however, the slave's first statement (39) was wrong and the latter statement proved to be correct (54), then the first claim would be invalidated, the note dismissed as spurious, and the defendant exonerated from the charge. In essence, if this negation of the first testimony (39) and the affirmation of the second testimony (54) could have been upheld, the presumption of guilt would have shifted from the defendant to the dead slave.

Antiphon pointed out that these opposing claims were further compounded by yet another charge, that the defendant committed the murder (68) and "took no partner when contriving the plot for his death" (§43). If this third claim against the defendant were true and the other two arguments false, then it would also cast doubt on the legitimacy of a "secret" note and encourage the dismissal of such evidence as unwarranted. Antiphon's rationale was to discredit the validity of all opposing claims by exposing that the following three charges were contradictory and could not possibly all be true: (1) that the defendant and slave were accomplices (39); (2) that the slave committed the murder independently of the accused (54); and (3) that the defendant committed the murder independently of the slave (68). Presenting these charges as not only incompatible but contradictory revealed such confusion in the prosecution's case that Antiphon rendered it impossible for his listeners to determine which charge was correct and the relationship of that correct charge to the authenticity of the note. By Platonic standards, such methods illustrate eristic discourse — the attempt to befuddle rather than to clarify. Yet, from a standard of relative perspective, probability and interpretation, such an argumentative technique was actually a rather sophisticated attempt to encourage the dismissal of all the prosecution's evidence as consisting of conflicting and unsubstantiated assertions.

After challenging the reliability of opposing witnesses, Antiphon concentrated his efforts on undermining the prosecution's motives by analyzing the efforts to distort the slave's testimony, invent the note, deny bail, and withhold a trial before the Areopagus. Understanding Antiphon's approach requires knowledge of the political climate at Athens, as well as the sentiments of Antiphon and his client. In 428 B.C. Mytilene (the major city of the island lesbos) had revolted from Athens, with the defendant's father taking an active part in the revolution (76). According to Jebb, the Athenian Herodes settled in Mytilene in 427 B.C., functioning as a territorial *kleruch* or a holder of allotted land (vol. 1, 56). This trial was held c. 414/413 B.C., only a short time before the revolt of Lesbos in 412 B.C.. Therefore, one can justly infer that Athens and Lesbos were hostile and that the Athenian *kleruchi* must have been very unpopular with the citizens of Lesbos. The Athenians would undoubtedly have been enraged by the murder of one of their compatriots by a man from Mytilene. In addition, Philostratus relates that Antiphon held no love for Athenian democracy (498) and has been regarded as "the brain of the oligarchic conspiracy" in 411 B.C. (*OCD* 74). Given these political affiliations, one can understand how Antiphon would champion a case providing an arena in which to challenge the political system he detested. One can also understand the contempt which the Athenians could have for Antiphon's client.

Antiphon's attempt to diminish politically based ill will was a major strategy in his advocacy. Such a strategy would later be labeled a case of *digressio*, or a section of an oration used to amplify some area not directly related to the subject, but helpful in persuading listeners (*De Inventione* 1. 97). Although Antiphon would not have been familiar with the term used later by Roman advocates such as Cicero, he did recognize the advantage of devoting a part of his plea toward gaining the good will of his listeners. Initially, Antiphon refuted opposing arguments while demonstrating that the accused possessed no motive for murdering Herodes. From this point forward, however, Antiphon mentioned numerous examples of homicide cases whose murderers had never been discovered (67–71). He pleaded for time, which, he said, "is a great thing for transferring judgment from violent emotion and to bring about the acquisition of truth" (72). Antiphon's delaying tactic was an attempt to cool public sentiment, which may have been putting undue pressure on the judges. The objective was to discourage a hasty decision provoked by political sentiment. The appeal for time was an attempt to create a dissociation between the actual issues and the larger emotional sentiment between the two city-states. This was an insightful use of *digressio* to re-establish the presumptions upon which a judgment ought to be reached.

Antiphon used a similar strategy when he had the accused shift from a defense of his own actions to the actions of his father during the revolution. He did not attempt to argue that the defendant's father did not participate in the revolt of 428 B.C. but rather revealed the circumstances which compelled the father to participate. Antiphon argued that "after these events" the defendant's father "did nothing wrong" (77) and would personally not have rebelled had he not been forced by the populace (79). According to Antiphon, the reason for the prosecutor's attack was simple: "this entire plot against me and him [the father] came about for the sake of money" (§79). Whether Antiphon believed that money was the key issue is unknown, but his strategy performed two important functions. First, it reduced and redirected the point at issue from political antagonisms between city-states to an individual economic dispute. Second, it portrayed a father's good, but misguided, intentions and a son's devotion. Using this plea as a sort of transition enabled Antiphon to shift from defensive refutation to offensive argument and provided the opportunity to establish verification of the defendant's innocence through the success of his religious sacrifices.

The defendant openly told his listeners that he withheld the strongest argument until the end, believing that the favorable signs from the gods "are my greatest evidence of proof that the charge brought against me by this man is without truth" (83). The modern reader is immediately tempted to dismiss the force of such utterances, but the emphasis and sincerity of the argument for Antiphon's contemporary listeners was substantial. Antiphon claimed to have supplied as much human evidence as possible, while the evidence of heavenly influence toward a just verdict was apparent in the defendant's successful sacrifices, safe voyages and the absence of ill-omens (82, 83). Dobson maintains that Antiphon sincerely believed that "the murdered man, if unavenged by human justice, will find divine champions who will not only bring homicide to book, but will punish the guilty city which has become polluted by harboring him" (33).

Establishing a line of advocacy which included deference to divine forces served to link a position based on probability with fundamental religious values. In this sense, only the immortal gods could know the sincerity of Antiphon's pleas, but if the judges were to reject these signs, they would be denying *dike* (justice), which was inherent in Athenian values and explicit in the operation of the legal system. Nevertheless, Antiphon recognized that he was not addressing gods, but his fellow Athenians. Consequently, his peroration was a final plea for a just verdict with the assurance that an ultimate, more equitable verdict would be reached by acquitting the defendant and thus bringing the case into the proper province of the Areopagus where traditional vows and procedures could be appropriately followed.

While *On the Murder of Herodes* reveals both strengths and weaknesses in Antiphon's forensic rhetoric, his attributes as the premier Athenian logographer are evident in the oration that he composed for his client. His argument that the charge of "wrong-doer" was inappropriate indicates a shrewd knowledge of the precepts of Athenian law and history as well as sensitivity to the current political situation. His treatment of the quality of witness-testimony under torture reveals proficiency in analysis. The use of probability (the inductive processes of *enumeratio* in particular) to establish a basis for such notions as "probable cause," "motive," "intent," and "presumption" is perhaps his most outstanding quality and one of the earliest applications of concepts central to forensic composition. The clarity and order of Antiphon's composition indicates a masterful incorporation of arguments which dissociate political sentiments from the case. Although his pleas are almost exclusively centered on probability, Antiphon skillfully interjected both witness-testimony and religious tenets into his writing.

Although Antiphon's emergence as the first prominent Athenian logographer allows critics to excuse some weaknesses, there are still faults which must be cited. The defendant for whom Antiphon composed the oration is known to have been young (80), yet the style of the speech bears the mark of an older, more sophisticated individual. If so, then Antiphon had not yet mastered the art of *ethopoeia*, or establishing the posture of the speaker within the oration — a characteristic for which Lysias would become famous. In addition, Antiphon centered his argument almost exclusively on the slave's evidence and often, as indicated, glossed over arguments of equal weight. It must be remembered, however, that Antiphon was experimenting, developing and teaching precepts of forensic oratory before Isocrates had left his teens and Plato had entered his boyhood. Even the most stringent historians of rhetoric should recognize Antiphon's pioneering attempts to establish and popularize theories that would later become the foundation for classical rhetoric in general and forensic oratory in particular. Antiphon's ability to write compositions for oral presentation illustrates the emergence of techniques that would later be systematized under the discipline of rhetoric and the close relationship between oral and written composition.

Rhetoric and the Isocratean School of Logography

> More than Plato, the Sophists, or other thinkers of his time, Isocrates appears to have realized the centrality of writing to effective thinking. His role in the advancement of writing as a pedagogical device has not received adequate scholarly attention (Kathleen E. Welch, "Writing Instruction in Ancient Athens after 450 B.C." in *A Short History of Writing Instruction*, 17).

In an earlier chapter, we mentioned that Isocrates' contributions to education were so important that some consider him to be nothing less than the father of humanism (Jaeger 1990). He benefitted from the knowledge of two previous generations of rhetoricians and incorporated and refined logography, or speech composition, into his curriculum, emphasizing its application as a tool for other disciplines. Through Isocrates' school, logography became a discipline of indispensable value — elevating the principles of rhetoric to a position of esteem in the areas of law, history and civic functions. Background information on both Isocrates and the emphasis of his educational system will help explain his concept of logography.

[Plutarch] tells us that Isocrates was the son of Theodorus of Erchia, a middle-class flutemaker (*Lives of the Ten Orators* 10. 836E). Isocrates was educated by some of the most influential scholars of his day: the rhetorician Theramenes, Gorgias of Leontini, Tisias from Syracuse, Prodicus of Ceos, and Socrates (*Lives of the Ten Orators* 836F). George Norlin emphasizes that Gorgias greatly influenced Isocrates in the areas of panhellenic themes and prose rhythm (Norlin vol. 1, xiii). William Mure asserts that Tisias, "unquestionably one of the greatest and most successful teachers of prose composition," also influenced Isocrates in the art of prose composition (96–97). Even Plato's continual carping criticisms of rhetoric were tempered when he spoke of that noble Isocrates, whom he claimed would become so superior in the study of rhetoric that he would make his predecessors seem like children (*Phaedrus* 279A). Isocrates, however, would receive his true fame not from his reputation as a student but as an educator.

Isocrates was without question the most illustrious teacher of his day. In at least two instances, Cicero regarded Isocrates as the master of all rhetoricians whose house became a training-school of eloquence for all Greece (*Brutus* 8. 32). Despite high fees (*Lives of the Ten Orators* 10. 837C, E), Isocrates had approximately one hundred pupils during his teaching career, usually no more than eight at one time (R. Johnson 28). Among these one hundred, of whom Jebb argued forty-one are known (vol. 2, 12), are some of the most socially influential individuals in fourth century B.C. Greece: Timotheos, Leodamas of Acharne, Lycurgus and Hypereides were prominent statesmen; philosophers and rhetoricians included Isaeos, Isocrates of Apollonia and Speusippos; and historical logographers including Ephoros, Theopompos and Androtion.

Greek city-states had a long history of internal warfare and colonization through domination. Relationships among cities were often done for purposes of alliance more than a sense of kinship or nationalism. The Isocratean school focused on one aim — to foster panhellenic statesmanship. Isocrates was committed to the notion of a united Greece and believed that rhetoric was a tool that empowered his educational system to promote such an ideal in a number of different areas. History, political science, geography, and ethics were joined with rhetorical studies and offered not for their own intrinsic educational value but were so taught, as R. Johnson argued, that Isocrates' school was a "school of political rhetoric" and "being ancillary to rhetorical compositions, the subjects were covered as composition required" (29). Isocrates' teaching methods were summarized by R. Johnson as: 1) instruction in the fundamentals of rhetoric; 2) the analysis of examples; 3) abundant practice in composition; 4) competition; and 5) group criticism (34). Thus, after presenting a composition to Isocrates, a student of history would conceivably be corrected not only on the logic and style of the work, but also on the moral tone of his thesis. To Isocrates, "none of the things which are done with intelligence take place without the aid of speech, but that all our actions as well as in all our thoughts speech is our guide, and is most employed by those who have the most wisdom" (*Antodosis* 2. 257). The practicality of Isocrates' school of rhetoric is best stated by Richard C. Jebb: "Isocrates was occupied . . . in developing a literary rhetoric, important, certainly, in its influence on the practical oratory of a later day, but of contemporary significance in the way of style *chiefly* for that Rhetorical school of history in which Ephoros and Theopompos are the earliest great names" (vol. 2, 72).

Cicero also stated that Isocrates directly influenced the historical writings of both Theopompos and Ephoros (*Orator* 49. 151; 51. 172). Ephoros and Theopompos, mentioned above as two historians from Isocrates' school, are illustrations of the integration of rhetoric into disciplines such as history. Isocrates' students were instructed in a system of logography which would try for historical accuracy, but never at the expense of diminishing the periodic rhythm of an eloquent moral plea. According to Quintilian (3. 4. 11), Isocrates held that praise and blame should be found in every kind of oratory — including logography. Therefore logography, wrote Chester G. Starr, "strongly under the influence of literary style and rhetorical development, could not consciously oppose the resulting tendencies which impelled them toward distortion; for truth . . . was not a fetish" (111). The works of Ephoros include a history of his home city Cyme, a work on style, and topical treatises on diverse information. The major contribution of Ephoros was his work on the history of Greece ('Ιστορίαι). The Greeks, as discussed above, had trouble maintaining even such war-prompted unions as the Delian Confederacy or the Peloponnesian League, let alone a type of national history in the strict sense. The uniqueness of Ephoros' work was the underlying theme of unity which attempted to identify Greek-speaking communities into a quasi-nationalistic oneness. Replete with sweeping condemnation and praise, Ephoros' prose was an attempt at a type of Homeric epic unity. In his analysis of Ephoros' writings, Bury has noticed the Isocratean influence in "the interruption of the narrative by moralizing platitudes; the introduction of elaborate Isocratean speeches, even when an army was facing the enemy; and the passion for panegyrics" (164). Influenced by such rhetoric, logography was designed to inspire action. Godfrey L. Barber also recognized this Isocratean influence and echoed Laquer's observation that a book of Ephoros is an excerpt from Isocrates, fully elaborated with historical and rhetorical detail (82, n.1).

Theopompos of Chios, the Spartan sympathizer and contemporary of Ephoros, is primarily famous for two works, his *Hellenica* (Ἑλληνικαὶ ἱστορίαι) and the *Philippica* (Φιλιππικά) (*OCD* 1059). Also affected by the nationalism of Isocrates, Theopompos saw Macedonia as the unifying force of Greece. Pearson pointed out that Theopompos also sacrificed credence for exaggerated rhetoric and moralizing (27). In brief, these new trends of fourth century B.C. logography under the Isocratean school of rhetoric responded to the taste of the public which Isocrates tried so desperately to educate. In the fourth century B.C., a man such as Isocrates could so refocus the Greek paideia that the medium itself became as important as the message. Even into the third century, logographers would disregard the relative objectivity of a fifth century B.C. Thucydides for the fourth-century embellishment fostered by Isocrates.

While Isocrates' school was no doubt impressive, its recognition should not lead to the belief that his emphasis on logography was representative of the popular practices of his contemporaries. Logography, as a system of prose composition, was important in all three branches of rhetoric: written composition (as in history), panegyric or epideictic oratory, and public speaking as exemplified in the law courts. The persuasive impact of historical logography permeated Hellenic culture, but the most dominant social effect of logography on ancient Greece was in the area of speech composition. It was in this latter area, the forensic or legal compositions of the courts, that sophists had their most pragmatic and pervasive form of logography. In fact, the technical compositions of forensic logography so dominated the study of rhetoric in the everyday affairs of Athenian life that Aristotle devoted part of the opening passages of his *Rhetoric* to criticizing its popularity and representation of rhetoric.

Despite Aristotle's criticisms, the popularity of forensic logography was understandable. Every Athenian citizen was compelled to represent himself in court and a practical need emerged to present the best prose composition for oral presentation in the law courts. Thus, speech composed for litigants to deliver orally in court was important not for lofty themes of morality advocated by Isocrates, but for the immediate goal of winning a court case. "Those who had no leisure or taste to become rhetoricians," wrote Jebb, "now began to find it worth while to buy their rhetoric ready made" (vol. 1, 3). As we have seen, the first representative of this profession at Athens was Antiphon; the first logographer in the sense of composing speeches for money (Jebb vol. 1, 3; *Lives of the Ten Orators* 10; Quintilian 3. 1. 11). In fact, Mure argued that Antiphon was the "inventor" of the art of public oratory, distinct from the literary orators of the sophists (103). Isocrates shared Aristotle's dislike for the "art" (ἡ τέχνη) of his contemporary logographers such as Antiphon, although Cicero wrote that Isocrates himself was once such a speech-writer but abandoned the practice (*Brutus* 12. 48).

In spite of Isocrates' opposition, the rise of professional speech-writers of forensic oratory, such as Lysias, popularized a shift in the meaning of logography from the more generic term of prose-composer to the more technical and specific forensic speech writer. The term logographer which once held a distinction associated little beyond Isocrates' one hundred students became popularized into the role of mass sophistic education of pragmatic civic functions. As George Kennedy stated, a logographer was now a man of "questionable respectability, unacceptable in intellectual and political circles" (1963, 177). Plato repeatedly used "logographer" (λογογράφος) as a term of reproach when discussing rhetoric (Plato, *Phaedrus* 257C, 257E, 258C, 264B). Logography, which represented the core of Isocratean paideia, had decayed into an amoral prostitution of rhetorical devices subordinating educational excellence for immediate, pragmatic success.

From the sixth to the fourth centuries B.C., the concept of

logography shifted meaning in direct correspondence with the varying social and intellectual movements of Greece. The sixth century logographer was an Ionian chronicler whose prose works rarely transcended reporting and often preserved many of the poetical and mythical characteristics of the epic narrative from which it slowly developed. In the fifth-century B.C., logography evolved from general prose literature to historical composition exemplified by Herodotus (Ionian tradition) and by Thucydides (Attic tradition). The growth in popularity of rhetoric in the late fifth and fourth centuries B.C. — particularly under the Isocratean school — resulted in another shift. The term "logographer" changed from the relative objectivity of Thucydides' historical composition to the panegyric morality of panhellenism which dominated the histories of Isocrates' students Ephoros and Theopompos. During the fourth century B.C., logography shifted again as the moralistic history of the Isocratean school yielded to the pragmatic sophistry of speech-composition for a price. The uses — and abuses — of rhetoric dictated both the quality and impact of logography as an emerging force shaping Hellenic culture.

The Sophistic Pollination of Rhetoric

> In its most creative period, that is when the great works of literature were produced, Greece was politically and linguistically fragmented. The "Greek language" was in fact a collection of local dialects which were used by separate city states in their public documents (L. R. Palmer, *The Greek Language*, 174).

Plato's stringent criticism of the intellectual merits of the Sicilian Sophistic, and rhetoric in general, took many forms. He disdained the expedient and pragmatic ends of the rhetoric taught by Gorgias and other sophists. He strongly opposed the forensic rhetoric promoted by expert logographers such as Antiphon and Lysias. He distrusted writing in general and "technical" logography in particular. These issues, and likely many others associated with the increasing popularity of rhetoric in Athens, were intensified by the competition between Plato, the sophists and Isocrates for the best students. Coupled with his obvious intellectual talents, Plato's status as an educator was doubtlessly enhanced by coming from an Athenian family of wealth and distinction, in marked contrast to non-Athenian sophists or foreign-educated Athenians such as Isocrates.

Plato, Aristotle and (even) Isocrates disparaged the achievements of sophists, leaving such an impression that, for centuries, Hellenic sophists were considered an intellectual embarrassment to the otherwise brilliant and lucid contributions that characterize Greece's Classical Period, particularly with respect to Athens' preeminent literary contributions. Centuries of scholars accepted the portrayal of sophists as opportunistic, glib and amoral. They were presumed to have had little or nothing to do with Greece's "literate revolution" (Havelock 1982) except to exploit writing for their own pragmatic, selfish purposes. Research in the last few decades, however, has largely amended this perception to the point that sophists are now recognized for significant cultural and artistic contributions.

The spreading popularity of sophistic rhetoric throughout Greece resulted in many significant contributions, a number of them before the time of Aristotle. One of the achievements of sophistic rhetoric was the written form of the Attic-Ionic dialect and, indirectly, its emergence as the substance of what we now consider Classical Greek. In the process of teaching rhetoric, itinerant sophists promoted the study of oratory, encouraged literacy through the teaching of writing, and indirectly contributed to the transformation of the Attic-Ionic dialect into a grapholect—the inscribed (and preferred) literary mode of Hellenic expression.

Efforts to re-evaluate sophistic contributions bring to light an important error. Categorizing all sophists as a single group underscores similarities but downplays differences. We have explored how sophistic rhetoric came from Sicily. However, in little more than one generation, rhetoric had diffused into a number of specialized applications, and the expansion of writing furthered the dissemination. Accounting for the diversity and complexity of sophistic discourse is difficult, but it offers a more sensitive understanding than thinking of sophists in a uniformly monolithic manner. This diversity itself is a tribute to the popularity of the sophistic movement. In a relatively brief period of time, sophists were known to come not only from Sicily but from all over the Greek-speaking world. Sophists who came to Athens frequently adapted their various dialects to the local Athenian (Attic) tongue, but they maintained their own techniques of composing. That is, as will be discussed later in more detail, sophists often changed over to the Attic dialect but kept the modalities of expression indigenous to their primary tongue.

Cultural and political forces help explain the impetus toward uniformity of literary expression. Athens, the oratorical and literary center of the Greek-speaking world, attracted and valued intellectuals. The Attic dialect, in turn, had assimilated features from other dialects — particularly the Ionic (Buck, 3), which had evolved as the oldest and most dominant form of expression for oral, epic poetry. So thoroughly did these two cultures and dialects mix (Herodotus 1. 56; Thucydides 6. 82; 7.57) that they became known as one: the Attic-Ionic dialect. The adoption of the Attic-Ionic dialect by prominent, respected individuals continuously empowered that dialect with the best thoughts and forms of expression from throughout the Hellenic world to the extent that it became the dialect of preference for writing (i.e. the grapholect). In the process of conforming to the Attic-Ionic dialect, sophists contributed not only their wisdom but also transferred their modes of expression. Various Greek dialects emphasized different genres and modes of expression, each carrying formulae that facilitated ways of shaping thought and expression. The incorporation of these modes of discourse into the Attic-Ionic dialect not only enhanced its nature but facilitated its literate evolution. Further, in the process of traveling throughout Greece, sophists helped greatly to establish the Attic-Ionic grapholect as the literary expression of choice.

Although the Attic-Ionic prose style has become synonymous with the literary efforts of classical Greece, it was actually in intellectual competition with other Greek dialects and was the beneficiary of many sophists who were themselves non-Athenian speakers. To examine only the testimony and fragments of sophistic discourse would result in the misconception that the Attic-Ionic dialect was the sole mode of expression and synonymous with what we now consider Classical Greek. How the spoken Attic-Ionic dialect emerged as the dominant form of written composition and the role that the sophists played in facilitating a virtual monopoly of literary expression with the Attic-Ionic dialect is largely unrecognized. In subject, form and transmission, sophistic rhetoric helped to solidify the literary form of Classical Greek.

In order to understand both the emergence of rhetoric and Hellenic literacy itself, we must acknowledge the influence and close relationship between oral and written composition. By tradition and preference, Plato and Aristotle were seen as the pinnacles of classical thought. Unfortunately, classical scholars assumed that

Plato and Aristotle were also the best representatives of an intellectual tradition and that their contemporaneous intellectuals, the sophists, were inferior in thought. This inference is understandable, particularly because it mirrors the sentiments of Plato and Aristotle, both of whom had stringent comments about their predecessors. As we have seen, however, Plato and Aristotle did not give accurate renderings of either the oral tradition which preceded them or the merits of the sophists whose technical logography rivaled their philosophical schools. Plato and Aristotle were early examples of literate minds and, therefore, unrepresentative of both their own contemporary and the historical intellectual climate. Their ability to utilize the advantages of literacy to foster abstract thinking free from the stylistic devices of oral composition used to facilitate memory was a turning point in the epistemology of discourse. Literacy provided much easier access to prosaic and hypotactic patterns of thought than grew out of the oral tradition which dominated pre-Socratic and sophistic thought. In short, Plato and Aristotle were critics of the sophistic tradition, a phenomenon which they only dimly understood in its context but did not hesitate to disparage.

The monumental contributions of Milman Parry and Albert B. Lord (1971) in demonstrating the complexities of Homeric, oral composition discussed earlier provide the paradigm for studying the relationship of oral and literate expression. Several contemporary classical scholars have begun to re-examine the sophists and to question the opinions of Plato and Aristotle. Untersteiner (1954), Segal (1962), Bowersock (1969), Guthrie (1971) and Kerferd (1981) established the continuity of sophistic thought with pre-Socratic philosophy, the sophistication of notions warranting serious philosophical inquiry, and the sustained tradition of the sophistic movement which flourished through Antiquity. Havelock's *Preface to Plato* (1963/1982) argued convincingly that conceptual processes growing out of the Homeric tradition and grounded in oral discourse were sophisticated in their own terms but (again) not by the restrictive standards of Plato. The contributions of these and other scholars compelled contemporary historians of rhetoric to recognize the oral nature of early Greek discourse and its complexity while recognizing that the sophists, as beneficiaries of this tradition, were refining their own composition processes in a manner different in nature and in kind from both Plato and Aristotle.

Sophistic Rhetoric and the Creation of a Hellenic Grapholect

It is important to recognize that Greek dialects did not result from the splintering of tongues from a single source, undergoing changes with the diffusion to new locations. Rather, they were a semi-autonomous but shared group of *oral* dialects. The "unification" of Hellenic languages was not the solidification of the spoken tongue. Rather, "Classical Greek" was a *literate* phenomenon, a confluence of dialects dominated by the Attic-Ionic forms resulting from efforts to create a literate language. The evolution from natural, oral dialects to the artificial written dialect was the result of a number of factors including social, cultural and political preferences. The sophists, as expert theoreticians and practitioners, were instrumental in not only its development but its dissemination throughout the Greek-speaking world.

The nature of Classical Greek masks an enormous diversity in orality which had significant implications for literary composition. The earliest evidence of a "Greek Language" (Palmer, 23), the Linear B fragments of the Bronze Age (c. 1200 B.C.), reveal a remarkable conformity across archaeological sites. However, the clay tablets of Linear B also reveal that the script was little more than what L. R. Palmer terms a "chancellery language" or a "fossilized administrative language" (53, 54) used for record keeping. The tablets did not represent the transcription of the oral language — any more than grocery lists would represent our speech. Excluding the uniformity of Linear B fragments, there is no evidence of a singular "Greek" language but rather a number of dialects which persisted throughout ancient Greece. Although it is quite probable that numerous oral dialects ceased to be spoken, were never preserved beyond the memory devices of oral composition and thus were forgotten, five major dialects evolved from oral discourse to written texts and thus preserved their features: Attic-Ionic, Arcado-Cyprian (Achaean), Aeolic, North West Greek, and Doric. These dialects, illustrated below, exhibited regional and cultural territoriality.

There are two important features to be noted from the diverse origins of the Greek language. First, and obviously, each dialect was rooted in oral discourse. Second, and less obvious, each came with identifiable traits indigenous to that mode of discourse. The Ionic and Attic dialects each had distinguishing characteristics but co-existed in their chief forms in a manner that greatly influenced writing; the reasons for this similarity will be discussed later.

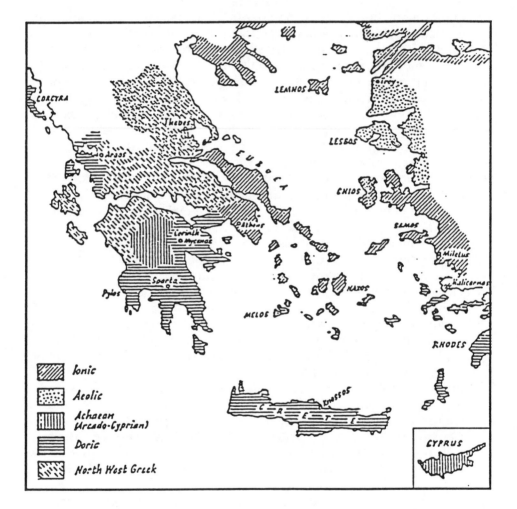

The legend reads:

- Ionic
- Aeolic
- Achaean (Arcado-Cyprian)
- Doric
- North West Greek

* Reproduced from L. R. Palmer's *The Greek Language* by permission of Faber & Faber

Despite the dialect elisions, apparent also in the Arcado-Cypriate group, this diversity persisted actively throughout the Classical Period, particularly when orality dominated composition and literacy was widely evident only in Athens, although it was beginning to emerge throughout Greece. Figure 5, extensively modified from a simpler diagram offered by Allen (1974, ix), illustrates this diversity.

The following figure illustrates that the principal dialects existed independent of a uniformly generic tongue. What is important to stress is that *during* the classical period, "Greek" meant a diversity of dialects marked by specific features of oral discourse. Classical Greek did not evolve from a single, indigenous and centralized tongue uttered initially at a single locale, transformed into script and then "frozen" as the classical language as was Latin (Allen, 1974, ix). Isolated by virtue of some of the most hilly terrain of the Mediterranean, multiple local dialects evolved throughout the Greek world. Some of these dialects came to be written and preserved. The eventual creation of a single "Classical Greek" was not the consequence of a uniform assimilation but rather of various linguistic, cultural and what is termed here "extra-rhetorical" features. As writing emerged and literacy became widespread, select features of dialects became incorporated into the dominant writing-dialect or the grapholect; that is, features of oral dialects that were considered effective and elegant were assimilated into the written style which became the *Koine* (Allen, 1974, viii), or common mode of literary expression. What was assimilated was not only unique words and phrases, which capture the surface features of dialects, but modal heuristics of thought and expression. That is, ways of structuring and composing ideas were transferred from the dialect into the grapholect. Eventually, Classical Greek became synonymous with the Attic-Ionic dialect, the dialect that constituted literary prose. Creation of this Classical Greek script, however, was the result of the confluence of these factors and one of the forces shaping this phenomenon were the sophists of the classical period. Their contribution, however, cannot be fully understood without understanding the nature of these dialects and the processes that helped to transform the Attic-Ionic dialect into the classical Greek script or *Koine*.

Hellenic Dialects and Sophistic Pollination

The five major dialects mentioned above evolved from oral discourse to written texts, and we thus have a record of their

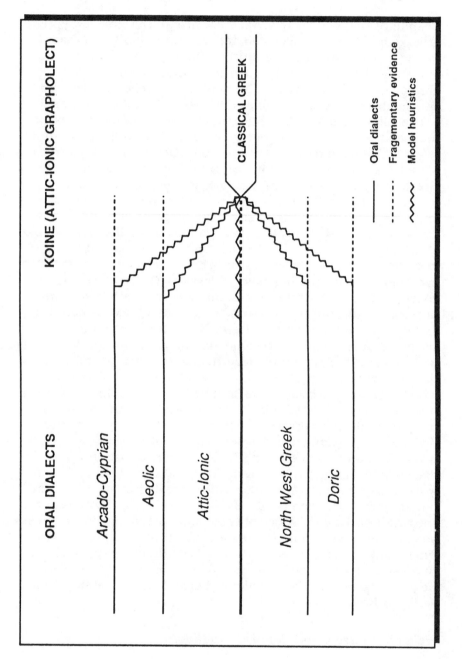

existence. Each dialect had its own unique linguistic properties, and each existed long before written language. Despite the natural interaction of people that results in borrowing and transference, each retained its chief features throughout the classical period. These features were distinguished primarily by their phonetic characteristics. While local terms and phrases doubtlessly existed, basic features of grammar, syntax, and vocabulary were generally shared. The salient and distinguishing oral feature of the dialects was the difference in sound patterns. The phonetic features of each dialect greatly contributed to its uniqueness and flavor, and the formulaic expressions that emerge were distinguished not only by nuances in their linguistic properties but by their tonal qualities as well.

The orality of Hellenic dialects offers insight that cannot be understood fully if we consider literary artifacts alone; that is, if we see evidence of composition solely from the literary texts which have survived. Hellenic dialects were distinguished in large part by their tonal features and, as Aristotle indicates in the *Rhetoric* (1403b), such stress was based on pitch. In fact, as Allen indicates, "tonal accent was one of the most characteristic phonetic features of ancient Greek" (118). An illustration will reveal the significance of this oral dimension. Greek dramatic literature was composed to be recited aloud. Pitch, one of the chief features in shaping meaning, is realized through oral renderings. Hearing Aristophanes *Birds*, as Stanford (102) indicates, is necessary to capture a dimension of the play's meaning. In saying the lines of the play in pitch, actors "chirp" their parts. No silent reading of the play, or even one whispered for that matter, would capture the oral orthography of its tonal features. The tonal features of discourse, as with a Gregorian chant, provide a facet of meaning beyond the words themselves. Alexandrian grammarians of the second century B.C. recognized this phenomenon and provided accent marks to help preserve the tonal pattern of ancient Greek; by the fourth century A.D., however, accent was altered in meaning when stress replaced tone and the oral quality of pitch was lost (Allen 1974, 114, 119).

While euphonic features of Greek dialects were lost even to ancient scholars, their impact on shaping Classical Greek was enormous, for tonal patterns shaped the formulae of the dialects. These formulae or modes of expression, in turn, served not only as aids to memory but also as ways to help compose thought. Issues of rhetoric discussed in dialogues such as the *Gorgias* and the *Phaedrus* reveal the sophistic concern with oral style, poetic patterns and tonal qualities. The earliest forms of literature were oral, and composing processes were shaped by the tonal patterns of the dialect. These patterns, in turn, facilitated configuration of thought similarly to how mnemonic devices of rhythm and cadence shaped memory and even creativity. Dialects, transmitted in part by sophists who travelled throughout the Greek-speaking world, helped to shape not only oral literature but also the conceptual modes that facilitated expression and eventually the scripts that insured their preservation.

As we have seen, one of the best examples of this "pollination" — one which even pre-dates sophistic influence — is the transmission of Homeric literature by rhapsodes (Palmer, 143–146). *Homerica* is primarily eastern Ionic, and the influence of the *Iliad* and the *Odyssey* throughout Greece established a dominance in expression that came to associate epic oral composition with the Ionic expression. The contributions of Hesiod, Pindar and Simonides further ingrained the Ionic dialect as the medium for poetic expression. Centuries of aoidoi and rhapsodes promoted and preserved the dialect as the mode for expressing great literature. It is important to stress that what became established as the medium of expression was not only the tonal features of the Ionic dialect but the formulaic patterns and modes of expression — in short, the heuristics of the dialect. Ionic became the first fully developed prose style. The range and flexibility of expression, from the historiography of Herodotus to the scientific/medical tracts of Hippocrates (*Corpus Hippocratium*), helped to associate the Ionic dialect with literate expression. Again, however, more was disseminated in Ionic literature than the tonal quality of the dialect. The formulaic techniques of composition plus the methods of analysis and inference in scientific and historical writing also were heuristics that were assimilated along with the oral orthography of the Ionic tongue.

The fruits of Ionic wisdom were naturally attractive to Athenians. In addition, social and cultural forces fostered an assimilation of the two dialects. In 494 B.C., Ionia fell to Persia. The once strong Greek leaders of the city-states of Ionia, who had so avidly sponsored and nurtured the arts of expression, fell or succumbed to "barbarian" tyranny. Lacking an atmosphere of patronage and sensing a climate of oppression, many Ionian artists and intellectuals welcomed the beneficence of Athens, who not only opposed Persian tyranny but offered the city as a school for Greek intellectuals (Thucydides 2. 41.1).

The pollination of Ionic forms and thought—so apparent in rhapsodic composition and in its harmonious compatibility with the Attic dialect—continued with the sophists of the classical period. Protagoras, an ardent traveler of the Greek world, was attracted to Athens. Unlike subsequent sophists, he persisted in writing in the Ionic dialect (Palmer, 154). As noted previously, his contributions to Athenian thought were probability and advantage, and his popularization of arguing from inference is well recognized in Plato's *Protagoras*. Many other thinkers who came from Ionia and other areas of Greece "Atticized" their dialect for Athenians. Despite modifications to Athenian discourse, sophists still transferred the modality of the expressions acquired in their native tongue (referred to in the earlier figure as the modal heuristic of the dialect). Gorgias of Leontini and Thrysamachus of Chalcedon (Asia Minor), for example, both wrote excellent Attic while transferring the poetic and periodic features of their respective grand and middle styles that had earned them fame in their "foreign" dialects (Palmer, 158). Thus, while sophists immigrated to Athens from throughout the Greek world and modified their discourse to Attic, they nonetheless transferred the modal heuristics endemic to their dialect onto the written Attic style, thus enriching the Attic-Ionic dialect with the most lucid modes of expression each dialect had to offer.

As discussed earlier, one of the best examples of a sophist influencing the Attic-Ionic style was Gorgias of Leontini. A number of ancient sources attest to Gorgias's impact on Athenian expression, and his popularity was most likely the motivating force driving Plato's *Gorgias*. Several ancient sources call particular and repeated attention not only to the substance of Gorgias's addresses and public performances but to the style of his expression. An acknowledged master of stylistic devices (*Schemata Gorgieia*), Gorgias was acclaimed for both his performance and teaching (Athenaeus 504E; Xenophon 2. 26; Norden, I, 63–79). Diodorus Siculus (12. 53. 1–4) notes the many rhetorical techniques Gorgias popularized with Athenians, who regarded him as a man of letters and paid handsomely to attend his school. Philostratus (*Epistula* 73; *Vitae Sophistarum* 1. 9. 3) provides convincing proof of Gorgias's impact on Athenian expression, citing how his style ("Gorgianize" [Γοργάξει]) influenced the expression of such prominent orators and writers as Pericles, Critias, and Thucydides. In fact, as Philostratus writes, "the detached phrases and approaches of Gorgias's discourse influenced many circles, particularly epic poets" (*Epistula* 73). Disparaged by Plato

(*Gorgias*), Aristophanes (*Aves* 1694; *Vespae* 420), and Aristotle (*Rhetoric* 1404a, 1406b), the impact that Gorgias made on the oral and literate style of the Attic-Ionic dialogue was nonetheless acknowledged through the time of Cicero (*Orator* 39, 165) and into the Second Sophistic. These testimonies of Gorgias's influence, coupled with fragments of his orations, reveal the nature and source of his influence on the Attic-Ionic grapholect.

Athenians were not without gifted stylists of their own, each of whom contributed to the sophistication of literate Attic expression. Thucydides, earlier mentioned as having been influenced by Gorgias's style and one of the great historians of Antiquity, is considered a master of Attic prose. His account of the Peloponnesian War became a model of literary expression as well as historiography. Similar examples from other forms of expression also contributed to the Attic literary style. The dramatic literature of playwrights such as Euripides, the masterpieces of Attic oratory by Antiphon and later Demosthenes helped to enshrine the Attic prose style as the medium of expression. Many literary scholars believe that Isocrates and his school of logography perfected Attic diction (Palmer, 148, 157, 169). In short, the assimilation and association of the Ionic dialect, the attraction which drew intellectuals from throughout Greece, and the local excellence of Athenian intellectuals all contributed toward the preeminence of the Attic-Ionic dialect. This distinction was enshrined not only by artful prose features but by the modal heuristics that facilitated the creation and conception of discourse. Most significant of all, and concomitant with the forces mentioned above, Athens became the first literate society of Greece.

The richness and sophistication of oral composition which gave preeminence to the Attic-Ionic dialect provided the heuristics for literary composition. As writing was popularized and reading became widespread, the techniques of oral composition assimilated from masters of other dialects complemented the contributions of Attic stylists to provide unparalleled written literature preserved for posterity. Eventually, techniques derived from oral composition were applied to literary composition, a phenomenon which George Kennedy (1980) popularized as *letteraturizzazione*. Through this process, in the terms of Walter J. Ong (1982), primary orality (the natural acquisition of speech) was systematized into principles of effective oral expression (primary rhetoric), from which some techniques are adopted to become principles for effective literary expression (secondary rhetoric) which, in turn, then become the standard for oral expression (secondary orality). The strong relationship between oral and literate expression is clear. The emergence and refinement of the Attic-Ionic literary style followed this evolution and was facilitated by sophistic rhetoric, as the following figure (Enos and Ackerman 1987) illustrates.

Social forces, in addition to literary phenomena, further helped to create an Attic-Ionic grapholect. The Ionic alphabet was made the official script (μεταγραμματισμός) in Athens in the archonship of Eucleides in 403–402 B.C. (Palmer, 96). Festivals such as the Panathenenaic and the great Dionysia provided both regular occasions for performances of literature and a spectacle for proficiency in the Attic dialect. Further, the distribution of Athenian policy in the form of epigraphical inscriptions doubtlessly assisted in both the spread and assimilation of the dialect throughout the empire. Eventually, Philip's conquest of the Hellenic world made his adoption of the Athenian dialect as the official language of Macedonia an imperially recognized form of literary expression (Welles, vii; Buck, 174–176; Palmer, 176). Social, political and intellectual forces contributed to the concentration of the Attic-Ionic dialect as the preferred literary mode of expression. Yet, even in their departure from native dialects, writers transferred the modal heuristics of style and argument that earned them initial recognition. Thus, the best features of other dialects became absorbed by the Attic-Ionic grapholect, which only further strengthened its position as the dominant mode of literary expression and, through the constant travel of sophists, was doubtlessly disseminated throughout Greece.

Hellenic discourse moved from a highly developed oral tradition to a literary medium in a relatively brief time. The features of the diverse Hellenic dialects provided the basis for understanding the evolution of the literate mode of Classical Greek. These events provide a context for understanding why Classical Greek was largely a confluence of the Attic and Ionic dialects and the role sophists played in its creation and transmission. First, Athenians readily assimilated the Ionic dialect with their own Atticism and thus conjoined the best and oldest of the oral literature of Greece with their own tongue. Second, Athens aggressively attracted the most eloquent thinkers from throughout Greece, and many of the most prominent stylists adapted to the Attic dialect while contributing some of the best heuristic features of their own dialects. The impact of Gorgias of Leontini, perhaps the most influential of all sophists, reveals the nature and extent of such influence on the

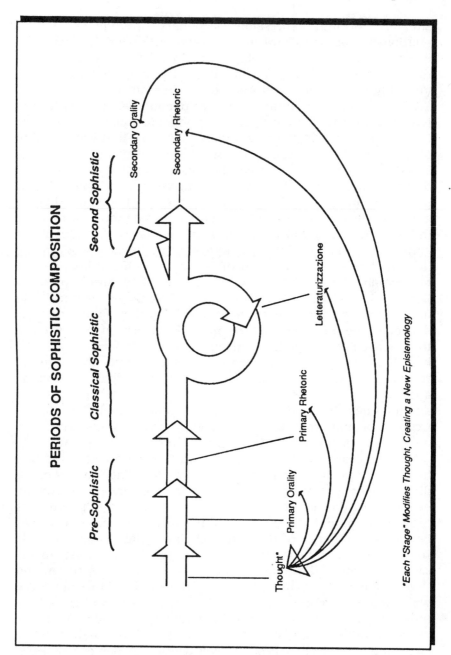

PERIODS OF SOPHISTIC COMPOSITION

Pre-Sophistic   Classical Sophistic   Second Sophistic

Primary Orality

Primary Rhetoric

Thought*

Letteraturizzazione

Secondary Orality

Secondary Rhetoric

*Each "Stage" Modifies Thought, Creating a New Epistemology

creation of a literate mode of expression. Third, as the first literate society of Greece, Athens transferred features of oral composition to the Attic script. This process of *letteraturizzazione* contributed directly to the emergence of Athens' literary process, which became the standard for written expression. Most importantly, when the Attic dialect was deemed official by Philip and later Roman conquerors, it established the Attic-Ionic dialect as the grapholect (in Ong's terms) that made the written script (Buck, 175) the *Koine* or recognized language of expression.

This phenomenon of oral and written composition was aided by several social and political forces which on the surface appear to be only tangential but were in actuality nothing less than a panhellenic phenomenon. There is little doubt that sophists were an enormous aid in establishing the *Koine* by enriching the Attic-Ionic dialect with their own techniques of composition and then transmitting that mode of expression throughout the Greek-speaking world. The factors of travel, the custom of mentor-apprentice education, the reliance on memory, the dissemination of oral literature to public audiences and the physiological characteristics necessary for such a lifestyle reveal that sophists were an important link in the transformation of oral and literate discourse. As an educational and cultural force, sophists were not only the medium for transmitting Hellenic literature but eventually for disseminating the Attic-Ionic dialect as the preferred tongue of artful expression. Thus, as writing shifted from an aid to memory to an art form, it is understandable why the Attic-Ionic dialect would dominate as the grapholect. The forces operating on the sophistic transmission of the Attic-Ionic dialect reveal features in the creation of a grapholect not readily apparent in an examination that concentrates solely on the literary artifacts. As a consequence, the principles of rhetoric which sophists promoted in oral expression became the foundation for literary expression and, in the process, established rhetoric as the basis for effective oral and written expression in the West.

Conclusion

This volume ends at the time when Aristotle opened his *Rhetoric* with a criticism of "technical writers." Aristotle's *Rhetoric* gave great attention to proofs (*pisteis*) leading to judgment (*krisis*) that provided good reasons (*phronesis*), ones which were even intended to justify emotive responses for auditors. Such attention to abstract rationality, however, is the consequence of a number of factors and does not adequately capture the evolution of forces that led to this disposition nor to the establishment of rhetoric itself. Readers should now have a context from which they can better make a judgement about Aristotle's remarks and ultimately about the *Rhetoric* itself. It should be apparent that the *Rhetoric* is a response to a long evolutionary phenomenon about the emerging consciousness of discourse and the eventual systematization of techniques to facilitate expression. Obviously such systems, particularly those which were formalized in Sicily into what would become the discipline of rhetoric, had great cultural and political implications, for they structured not only the expression of ideas but the ideas themselves.

There are a number of important observations about rhetoric before Aristotle. It is clear that the earliest notions of discourse were vague and general; there was little recognition of a specialization of topic or genre. Ideas of creativity in discourse ranged from divine inspiration to individual cunning. While the notion of divine insight, particularly evident with the rhapsodes, lasted beyond the Homeric period, the consciousness of discourse coincided with the invention of abstract systems that facilitated expression. Much of this was driven by an art directed toward pragmatic expression; systems of discourse in such areas as poetry, oratory and history were invented to facilitate these forms of expression. Notions of rhetoric, occurring within these developing fields, refined procedures and defined standards of judgment. Yet, these notions of what constituted the composition of effective discourse were driven by forces which were not limited to rationality.

Homeric discourse was celebratory and ceremonial. The discourse embraced occasions — actual or otherwise — and drew from those events a code of morality. Even at this early stage the signs of systematic composition were clear. Nonliterate aoidoi spoke their tales aided by formulaic patterns that facilitated expression and aided memory. These patterns were echoed by the literate aoidoi and their recorded *Homerica*. The teaching of such composition, passed down from mentor to apprentice, refined systems of expression that evolved into the genre of rhapsodic composition. The rhapsodic tradition attempted to systematize the preservation of both oral and written literature. Attention to what constitutes meaning and how it is formed reveals a level of consciousness that prompted abstraction of principles. This level of discourse was epideictic, and its context prescribed certain genre-expectations that themselves became an agenda for the techniques of composition.

Driven by pragmatic needs of legal and civic affairs, specialized discourse evolved that modified earlier systems of oral and written expression, giving birth to logography. With Herodotus and the logographers who preceded him, we witnessed the evolution of rhetoric from a rhapsodic tradition of tale-telling of heroic events to the chronicling of human phenomena. Herodotus advanced beyond his predecessors by providing reasons that explained how and why events of human action took place. In his account of the Battle of Marathon, Herodotus "argued" for an interpretation of history. He applied rhetorical principles to reach an interpretation rather than a simple chronicling of events. In the tradition of earlier rhapsodes and logographers, Herodotus's use of rhetoric spanned principles of composition to principles of argumentation. These techniques provided a foundation which viewed discourse as a process — a viewpoint that would lead to the establishment of rhetoric as a discipline.

Democracy intensified specialization in the arts of expression. Logography had great instrumental value for law and civic matters. In response to those needs, experts in speech-composition emerged. The source of power provided by these systems of expression was apparent both in Sicily and Athens. Rhetoric emerged from this confluence of the pragmatic and intellectual, the artistic and functional. As a discipline, rhetoric offered artful expression with an expedient purpose, a system whose power came not only from the cogency of ideas but also from the eloquent ways in which those ideas were expressed. Rhetoric represented the artful expression of wisdom and offered educational systems for achieving effective oral and written expression. The following figure illustrates this evolution of notions about discourse.

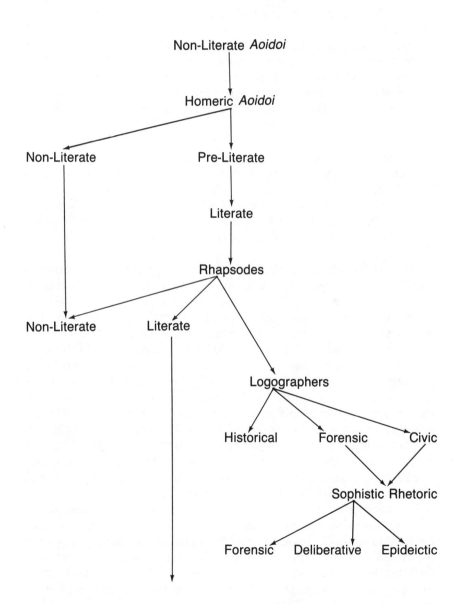

As we have seen, the motives for the study of rhetoric were often pragmatic instead of purely intellectual. Democracy provided the context that made rhetoric a source of social power. This force in rhetoric prompted a blossoming of attention to discourse that moved from the poetic to the practical. The requirements for proficiency in political and legal contexts also prompted specialization in techniques. The pre-Socratic views of Empedocles on probability, relativism and sense-perception had fostered ideas that Corax and Tisias systematized into the creation of the discipline of rhetoric. The birth of rhetoric in Sicily, nurtured by the political and social forces of the time, was actually an evolution of thought in communities where discourse was a source of power. This condition was true for periods of time in Sicily and in Athens, whose more firmly established democracy provided the stability for schools of rhetoric. This philosophy of education in democracies nurtured the rise of sophists who thrived in both personal performance and teaching others the instrumental power of proficient discourse. Sophistic influence became so endemic and pervasive that its mode of teaching, including rhetoric, became synonymous with higher education.

Plato's opposition to sophistic rhetoric, as we have seen, centered on what he believed to be its harmful impact on the administration of civic and legal affairs and the training of youth. Gorgias of Leontini was well known in Athens from the time of Socrates and was a rival for students and education methods. The *Gorgias* portrays his student, Polus, as a youthful participant. At the time of the actual composition of the *Gorgias*, Polus had probably established his school of rhetoric in Southern Italy and continued to enhance the reputation of the rhetoric of his mentor. Later, in the *Phaedrus*, the threat and rivalry of Sicilian rhetoric to Plato is still evident. Lysias, to a lesser extent, is another opponent of Socrates and, in the *Phaedrus*, he represents the popular logographer disparaged by Plato. Plato's Athens was a dynamic and intellectually stimulating community. Strong opposing views of rhetoric were contributing factors to the stimulation.

The coherence of Sicilian rhetoric is evident in the generations of rhetoricians who followed Empedocles, Corax and Tisias. Gorgias became immensely popular in Athens and, eventually, throughout the Hellenic world. Polus continued that tradition in Southern Italy and Lysias established himself in Athens with a successful career in logography. The sustained impact was most clearly evident in the notion of "schools" of rhetoric. The Sicilian Sophists established rhetoric as a system of serious study and made it endemic in their notion of paideia. The Sicilian Sophistic established itself as a viable educational force not only on its own island but, with the itinerant movement of sophists, in Athens and the Greek-speaking world. Competing schools of rhetoric prospered but their impact, relative to the Sicilian Sophistic, must be qualified. While Plato, Aristotle and Isocrates all were openly opposed to the rhetoric of the Sicilian Sophistic, their views of rhetoric (which differed from each other as well as from the sophists) had a far lesser impact. Individuals were drawn to Athens from all over the Greek world to attend the schools of Plato, Isocrates, and Aristotle. In fact, Aristotle himself first came to Athens to study under Plato before establishing his own school. Despite their attraction, the impact of these schools was (with some qualification) limited to those who came to Athens. Sophists, on the other hand, travelled throughout the Greek world and would continue to expand their impact even into the Roman Empire.

The intellectual impact of Plato, Isocrates and Aristotle on rhetoric is undeniable, and we should be cautious not to confuse the popularity of the sophistic movement with its intellectual merit. However, we also should not hesitate to credit a system which helped to resolve problems and arrive at choices in an alternative manner to the tyranny and arbitrary procedures with which many of the critical decisions influencing ancient history appear to have been made. As a system stressing probable judgment and recognizing the role of emotivism in discourse, the Sicilian Sophistic proved itself to be a cultural force unmatched by any other educational discipline of its time. In longevity and breadth of impact, the discipline of rhetoric conceived in Sicily and developed throughout the Hellenic world was far more pervasive than those which came forth from the Academy of Plato, the Peripatetic School of Aristotle or even the Isocratean school of Humanism.

Aristotle's *Rhetoric* was meant to challenge but not to crush the rhetoric of the sophists out of existence as his teacher Plato had sought. Aristotle's intent was to provide a better version of rhetoric than the sophists offered—one worthy of a philosopher's notion of paideia. He hoped to show that rhetoric, as created and popularized, was not all that it could have been. Aristotle sought to present a view of rhetoric that would be both functional and compatible with the standards of a serious discipline. As Havelock argued in *Preface to Plato*, the sophists had shifted the notion of paideia from its Homeric center to a new degree of consciousness about the human capacity. Here we see that the popularity of their rhetoric had provided the evolution of a mentality and process of discourse that made the creation of rhetoric as a discipline possible. Aristotle's efforts to decenter the meaning of rhetoric from its sophistic orientation is as much a statement about its impact as it is of his opposition. In this respect, the introduction to Aristotle's *Rhetoric* ought to be seen not as opening remarks but rather as a response to and commentary upon the centuries-long evolution of thought and expression that lead to the creation of rhetoric. He sought to redirect that rhetoric by articulating one of the most important texts ever created in the discipline's history. Although the *Rhetoric*'s impact is unassailable, it was a response to a pervasive notion of rhetoric that evolved over centuries and would flourish for centuries more. His monumental work should not be seen as a starting point in the history of rhetoric but rather as a response to a pre-history.

When Susanne K. Langer discussed language in *Philosophy in a New Key* (126–143) she argued that discursive thought gives rise to science but that nondiscursive thought provides the heuristics to construct a theory of understanding art. "The parent stock of both conceptual types," Langer argued, "of verbal and non-verbal formulation, is the basic human act of symbolic transformation" (143). In much the same spirit as Langer's observations, notions of rhetoric which predate Platonic and Aristotelian rationalism need not, by default, be labeled "irrational" or "atheoretical" but rather nonrational, systematic procedures for symbolizing thoughts and sentiments. Aristotle's account of the nature of rhetoric — and dismissal of earlier efforts — distorts the history of the discipline. The presumptions upon which Aristotle establishes rhetoric as a techne are a disservice to earlier artistic and intellectual contributions, particularly the Sicilian Sophistic, advance restrictive claims about knowledge and its acquisition, and posit an unwarranted incompatibility between rationality and style. The observations made in this work prompt us to review the notion that rhetoric is a revolutionary new discipline grounded in rationality, replacing it with the view that Aristotle's notion of rhetoric is yet another illustration of a powerful evolutionary paradigm growing out of a well-established context. Despite the unquestioned power and sustained popularity of Aristotle's *Rhetoric*, it is clear that his view was not the sole perspective but rather a competing view contesting the enormous popularity of sophistic rhetoric. The characterization of the sophists presented in this text links Homeric, rhapsodic and logographic antecedents with the demonstrable contributions of the sophists to the cumulative, evolutionary path of rhetoric as a discipline. In establishing the relationship of rhetoric to the society in which it occurred, this text sought to emphasize that relationship as a central force in the development of rhetoric.

Lastly, we should reconsider the relationship between orality and literacy as well as the relationship between rhetoric and composition. The primacy of oral systems of rhetoric, their overwhelming pervasiveness and sustained popularity, is undeniable. Yet writing and, in particular the development of logography, had a vital impact on the evolution of rhetoric. Writing, refined under the artistic and pragmatic benefits of logography, made the advantages of stable, unchanging communication obvious— benefits unafforded by the immediate and momentary advantages of oral rhetoric. The close relationship between speaking and writing, and their inextricable relationship to thought, expanded rhetoric to include writing as a natural complement to oral rhetoric. Sophists promoted the advantages of both oral and written rhetoric for artistic and pragmatic needs, further reinforcing their close relationship. *Letteraturizzazione* was not a dramatic event but rather a gradually emerging consequence of social, cultural and intellectual forces. The solidification of rhetoric occurred with the popularization of writing through logography. The sophists were the primary agents of such development, for their systems of oral and written rhetoric facilitated heightened sensitivity to the processes of expression and a keener consciousness of the relationship between cognition and expression in social interaction than had existed before.

Techniques of composition, oral and written, preceded rhetoric and were interactive. Rhapsodes, historians, orators and logographers demonstrated a compatible and correlative relationship between oral and written composition long before systems of rhetoric were formalized. To think that when rhetoric reached the status of a discipline in the fifth century B.C. its nature was oral and that writing systems were subsequent (and derivative) is to ignore centuries of the interrelated evolution of oral and written composition that provided the heuristics that made rhetoric systematic and (therefore) disciplinary. Ancient Greeks saw applications of rhetoric for both oral and written expression not as accidental but rather as consequential; for all practical purposes, they viewed the relationship as univocal. Plato's well known fear of writing was not, by default, a proclamation solely for orality. It was an effort to create a dissociation between oral and written expression. Sophists resisted severing orality from literacy as Plato advocated. The sophists' sustained influence is testimony to the merits of rhetoric's contributions to the marriage of oral and written composition. Their perpetuation of that relationship, however, was a continuation of a bonding that had been formed long before rhetoric emerged as a discipline.

Works Consulted

Primary Sources

Abbreviations Used

RG *Rhetores Graeci*—see listing under this title.
D-K *Die Fragmente der Vorsokratiker*—see listing under this title.
EM Epigraphical Museum (Athens)—a code for volumes containing inscriptions.
OCD *Oxford Classical Dictionary*—see listing under this title.

[Anaximenes]. *Rhetorica ad Alexandrum.*
[_____]. Ἀνωνύμου ἐπίτομὴ ῥητορικῆς. *RG*, vol. 3, 610, 611.
Antiphon. *Fragmenta.*
_____. *On the Murder of Herodes.* Aristophanes. *Acharnenses.*
_____. *Aves.*
_____. *Vespae.*
Aristotle. *Athenian Constitution.*
_____. *Metaphysics.*
_____. *Ethica Nicomachea.*
_____. *Poetics.*
_____. *Rhetoric.*
_____. *Sophistici Elenchi.*
_____. *Topica.*
[Aristotle]. *De Melisso, Xenophane, Gorgias.*
"Artium scriptores: Reste der voraristotelischen Rhetorik." *Österreichische Akademie der Wissenschaften, Philosophisch-historische Klasse, Sitzungsberichte,* 227. Ed. Ludwig Radermacher. Band 3. Vienna: Rudolf M. Rohrer, 1951, 28–35.
Athenaeus. *Deipnosophistae.*
_____. *Scholia.*
Callimachis. *Fragmenta.*
Cicero. *Brutus.*
_____. *De Inventione.*
_____. *De Oratore.*
_____. *Orator.*
[_____]. *Rhetorica ad Herennium.*
Clemens Alexandrinus. *Stomateis.*

Die Fragmente der Vorsokratiker (D-K). Eds. Hermann Diels and Walther Kranz. Three volumes. Dublin: Weidmann, 1972.

Diodorus Siculus.

Diogenes Laertius. *Vitae Philosophorum.*

Diogenianus. *Paroemiae.*

Dionysius Halicarnassus. *De compositione verborum.*

_____. *De Imitatione.*

_____. *De Isocrate.*

_____. *De Lysia.*

_____. *De Thucydide.*

_____. *Epistula ad Pompeium.*

Dionysius Thrax. Τέχνη γραμματική (with scholia). In *Dionysii Thracis Ares Grammatica.* Ed. Gustavus Vhig. Lipsiae: B. G. Teubner, 1833.

Doxopatrus. Προλέγομενα τῆς ῥητορικῆς. *RG,* vol. 6, 12–14.

_____. Ὁμιλίαι εἰς ᾽Αφθονίου προγυμνάσματα. *RG,* vol. 2, 119, 140.

Eunapius. *Lives of the Philosophers.*

Gorgias. *Epitaphios.*

_____. *Helen.*

_____. *Palamedes.*

Herodotus. *The Persian Wars.*

Hesiod. *Erga.*

_____. *Fragmenta Dubia.* or *Incertae Sedes Fragmenta.*

_____. *Theogonia.*

Homer. *Iliad.*

_____. *Odyssey.*

[*Homerica*], *Of the Origin of Homer and Hesiod, and Their Contest.*

Inscriptiones Atticae: Evclidis Anno Anteriores. 1 (2). 52 (p. 23); EM 6855. Chicago: Ares Publishers Inc., 1984.

Inscriptiones Graecae: Megaridis Oropiae Boetiae. First volume. Ed. Gvilelmvs Dittenberger. Berolini: Apvd Georgivm Reimervm, 1892.

Isocrates. *Against the Sophists.*

_____. *Antidosis.*

_____. *Helen.*

_____. *Panegyricus.*

Josephus. *Contra Apionem.*

Kritias. "Poetische Fragmente." D-K 88. B2.

Lucian. *Herodotus.*

Lycurgus. *Contra Leocratem.*

A Manual of Greek Historical Inscriptions. Eds. E. L. Hicks and G. F. Hill. Oxford: Clarendon Press, 1901.

Maximus Planudae. Προλέγομενα τῆς ῥητορικῆς. *RG,* vol. 5, 215, 216.

The Older Sophists. Ed. Rosamond Kent Sprague. Revised edition. Columbia SC: University of South Carolina Press, 1990.

Pausanias.

Philostratus. *Vitae Sophistarum.*

Philostratus. *Epistula.*
Pindar. *Isthmian Odes.*
_____. *Nemean Odes.*
_____. *Olympian Odes.*
_____. *Pythian Odes.*
Plato. *Apologia.*
_____. *Euthydemus.*
_____. *Gorgias: A Revised Text with Introduction and Commentary.* Ed.
    E. R. Dodds. Oxford: Clarendon Press, 1971.
_____. *Hipparchus.*
_____. *Ion.*
_____. *Leges.*
_____. *Lysis.*
_____. *Menexenus.*
_____. *Meno.*
_____. *Parmenides.*
_____. *Phaedo.*
_____. *Phaedrus.*
_____. *Protagoras.*
_____. *Sophist.*
_____. *Timaeus.*
Plutarch. *Vitae decem oratorum: Lysias.*
_____. *Vitae decem oratorum: Isocrates.*
_____. *De Malignitate Herodoti [Moralia].*
_____. *Vitae Parallelae: Aristides.*
_____. *Vitae Parallelae: Pericles.*
_____. *Vitae Parallelae: Themistocles.*
[Plutarch]. Προλέγομενα τῶν στάσεων. *RG*, vol. 7.1, p. 6.
_____. *Vita Homeri.*
Quintilian. *Institutio oratoria.*
Rhetores Graeci (RG). Ed. Christianus Walz. Vols. 1–8. Osnabruck: Otto
    Zeller, 1968 (reproductio phototypica editionis 1832–1836).
*A Selection of Greek Historical Inscriptions to the End of the Fifth Century
    B.C.* Ed. Marcus N. Tod. Second edition. Oxford: Clarendon Press, 1946.
Sextus Empiricus. *Against the Logicians.*
_____. *Against the Professors.*
_____. *Against the Rhetoricians.*
Simplicius. *Aristotelis de Physica Commentarii.*
Sophocles. *Oedipus Tyrannus.*
Sopatus. Προλέγομενα τῆς Ἐρμογένους ῥητορικῆς. *RG*, vol. 4, 11–14, 19.
_____. Σωπάτρου εἰs τὴν Ἐρμογένουs τέχνην. *RG*, vol. 5, 6, 7, 65.
Strabo.
Sylloge Inscriptiones Graecarum. Ed. Guilelmo Dittenberger. Volumes
    I–III.. Fourth edition. Hildesheim: Georg Olms-Verlagsbuchhandlung,
    1960.

Syrianus, Sopatrus and Marcellinus. Σωπάτρου εἰς στάσεις τοῦ Ἑρμογένους. *RG*, vol. 4, [159], 575.

Theophrastus. *De Sensu*.

Thucydides. *The Peloponnesian War*.

Troilus. Προλέγομενα τῆς ῥητορικῆς Ἑρμογένους. *RG*, vol. 6, 48, 49.

Thesaurus Linguae Graecae: Canon of Greek Authors and Works. Eds. Luci Berkowitz and Karl A. Squitier. Third edition. New York and Oxford: Oxford University Press, 1990.

Xenophon. *Anabasis*.

_____. *Memorabilia.*

_____. *Symposium*.

Secondary Sources

Allen, T. W. "Pisistratus and Homer." *Classical Quarterly*, 7 (1913): 33–51.

Allen, W. Sidney. *Accent and Rhythm — Prosodic Features of Latin and Greek: A Study in Theory and Reconstruction*. Cambridge: Cambridge University Press, 1973.

_____. *Vox Graeca: The Pronunciation of Classical Greek*. Second edition. Cambridge: Cambridge University Press, 1973.

Andrews, A. *The Greek Tyrants*. New York: Harper & Row, Publishers, 1963.

Arnhart, Larry. *Aristotle on Political Reasoning: A Commentary on the "Rhetoric."* DeKalb, IL: Northern Illinois University Press, 1981.

Avotins, I. "The Holders of the Chairs of Rhetoric at Athens." *Harvard Studies in Classical Philology*, 79 (1975): 313–324.

Bahn, Eugene. "Interpretative Reading in Ancient Greece." *Quarterly Journal of Speech*, 18 (1932): 432–440.

Bahn, Eugene and Margaret L. Bahn. *A History of Oral Interpretation*. Minneapolis: Burgess Publishing Co., 1970.

Barber, Godfrey Louis. *The Historian Ephorus*. Cambridge: The University Press, 1935.

Barwick, Karl. "Die Gliederung der rhetorischen Τέχνη und die horazische Epistula ad Pisones." *Hermes*, 57 (1922): 1–62.

Boardman, John. *The Greeks Overseas*. Baltimore: Penguin Books, 1964.

Bonner, Robert J. *Evidence in Athenian Courts*. Chicago: University of Chicago Press, 1905.

_____. *Lawyers and Litigants in Ancient Athens, the Genesis of the Legal Profession*. Chicago: The University of Chicago Press, 1927.

Bonner, Stanley F. *The Literary Treatises of Dionysius of Halicarnassus: A Study in the Development of the Critical Method*. Cambridge: The University Press, 1939.

Bowersock, G. W. *Greek Sophists in the Roman Empire*. Oxford: Clarendon Press, 1969.

Buck, C. D. *The Greek Dialects.* Chicago: University of Chicago Press, 1955.

Burn, Andrew Robert. *Persia and the Greeks: The Defense of the West, c. 546–478 B.C.* London: E. Arnold, 1962.

Bury, J. B. *The Ancient Greek Historians.* New York: Dover Publications, Inc., 1958.

Calhoun, George Miller. "Oral and Written Pleading in Athenian Courts." *Transactions and Proceedings of the American Philological Association,* 49 (1919): 177–193.

Caven, Brian. *Dionysius I: War-Lord of Sicily.* New Haven, CT: Yale University Press, 1990.

Chroust, Anton-Hermann. "Aristotle's First Literary Effort: The Gryllus, A Lost Dialogue on the Nature of Rhetoric." In *Aristotle: The Classical Heritage of Rhetoric,* edited by Keith V. Erickson. Metuchen, NJ: The Scarecrow Press, Inc., 1974.

Clark, Donald Lemen. *Rhetoric in Greco-Roman Education.* New York: Columbia University Press, 1966.

Cole, Thomas. *The Origins of Rhetoric in Ancient Greece.* Baltimore: Johns Hopkins University Press, 1991.

———. "Who Was Corax?" Unpublished essay.

Conley, Thomas M. *Rhetoric in the European Tradition.* New York: Longman Publishing Group, 1990.

Cope, E. M. *An Introduction to Aristotle's* Rhetoric *with Analysis, Notes and Appendices.* London: Macmillan and Co., 1867.

Crem, Theresa. "The Definition of Rhetoric According to Aristotle." In *Aristotle: The Classical Heritage of Rhetoric,* edited by Keith V. Erickson. Metuchen, NJ: The Scarecrow Press. 1974.

Davidson, J. A. "The Homeric Question." In *A Companion to Homer,* edited by Alan J. B. Wace and Frank H. Stubbings. New York: Macmillian Publishing Co., Inc., 1969.

———. "The Transmission of the Text." In *A Companion to Homer,* edited by Alan J. B. Wace and Frank H. Stubbins. New York: Macmillan Publishing Co., 1969.

de Romilly, Jacqueline. *Magic and Rhetoric in Ancient Greece.* Cambridge, MA: Harvard University Press, 1975.

Diels, Hermann. "Gorgias und Empedokles." *Sitzungsberichte der Königlich Preussischen Akademie der Wissenschaften zu Berlin* 18 (1884): 343–368.

Dobson, John F. *The Greek Orators.* Freeport, NY: Books for Libraries Press, 1971.

Dodds, E. R. *The Greeks and the Irrational.* Berkeley, CA: University of California Press, 1973.

———. "Homer: Homer as Oral Poetry." In *Fifty Years (and Twelve) of Classical Scholarship,* edited by Maurice Platnauer. Oxford: Basil Blackwell, 1968.

Dover, K. J. "The Chronology of Antiphon's Speeches." *Classical Quarterly*, 44 (1950): 44–60.

Dunbabin, T. J. *The Western Greeks*. Oxford: Clarendon Press, 1948.

Engell, Richard. "Implications for Communication of the Rhetorical Epistemology of Gorgias of Leontini." Western Speech, 37 (1973): 175–184.

Enos, Richard Leo. "Aristotle, Empedocles and the Notion of Rhetoric." In *In Search of Justice: The Indiana Tradition in Speech Communication*, edited by Richard J. Jensen and John C. Hammerback. Amsterdam: Rodopi, 1987.

_____. "The Art of Rhetoric at the Amphiareion of Oropos: A Study of Epigraphical Evidence as Written Communication." *Written Communication*, 3 (January 1986): 3–14.

_____. "The Effects of Imperial Patronage on the Rhetorical Tradition of the Athenian Second Sophistic." *Communication Quarterly*, 25 (1977): 3–10.

_____. "Emerging Notions of Heuristic, Eristic, and Protreptic Rhetoric in Homeric Discourse: Proto-Literate Conniving, Wrangling and Reasoning." In *Selected Papers From the 1981 Texas Writing Research Conference*, edited by Maxine C. Hairston and Cynthia L. Selfe, 44–64. Austin: University of Texas at Austin, 1981.

_____. "The Epistemology of Gorgias' Rhetoric: A Re-examination." Southern Speech Communication Journal, 42 (Fall 1976): 35–51.

_____. "The Hellenic Rhapsode." *Western Journal of Speech Communication*, 42 (Spring 1978): 134–143.

_____. "Notions, Presumptions, and Presuppositions in Hellenic Discourse: Rhetorical Theory as Philological Evidence." *Philosophy and Rhetoric*, 14 (1981): 173–184.

_____. "The Persuasive and Social Force of Logography in Ancient Greece." Central States Speech Journal, 25 (1974): 4–10.

_____. "Review of Pietro Pucci, *Hesiod and the Language of Poetry*." *Rhetoric Society Quarterly*, 10 (Winter 1980): 38–40.

_____. "Rhetorical Intent in Ancient Historiography: Herodotus and the Battle of Marathon." *Communication Quarterly*, 24 (1976): 24–31.

_____. "Sophistic Formulae and the Emergence of the Attic-Ionic Grapholect: A Study in Oral and Written Communication." In *Oral and Written Communication: Historical Approaches*, edited by Richard Leo Enos. Newbury Park CA: Sage Publications, 1990.

Enos, Richard Leo and John Ackerman. "*Letteraturizzazione* and Hellenic Rhetoric: An Analysis for Research with Extensions." In *Visions of Rhetoric: History, Theory and Criticism*, edited by Charles W. Kneupper. Arlington, TX: Rhetoric Society of America, 1987.

Enos, Richard Leo and Janice Lauer. "The Meaning of 'Heuristic' in Aristotle's Rhetoric and Its Implications for Contemporary Rhetorical Theory." In *A Rhetoric of Doing: Essays Honoring James L. Kinneavy*, edited by Stephen P. Witte, Neil Nakadate, and Roger D. Cherry. Carbondale: Southern Illinois University Press, 1992.

Erickson, Keith V. "The Lost Rhetorics of Aristotle." *Communication Monographs*, 43 (1976): 229–237.

Fairbank, Alfred. *The Story of Handwriting: Origins and Development.* New York: Watson-Guptill, 1970.

Finley, John H., Jr. *Thucydides.* Ann Arbor: The University of Michigan Press, 1967.

Finley, M. I. *A History of Sicily: Ancient Sicily.* New York: The Viking Press, 1968.

Freeman, Edward A. *The History of Sicily*, four vols. Oxford: Clarendon Press, 1891–1894.

Freeman, Kathleen. *Ancilla to the Pre-Socratic Philosophers.* Oxford: Basil Blackwell, 1971.

_____. *The Murder of Herodes and Other Trials from the Athenian Law Courts.* New York: W. W. Norton & Company, 1963.

_____. *The Pre-Socratic Philosophers: A Companion to Diels, Fragmente der Vorsokratiker*, 2nd ed. Oxford: Basil Blackwell, 1966.

Friedlander, Paul. "Plato." Translated by H. Meyerhoff. Reprinted in: *Plato: True and Sophistic Rhetoric*, edited by K. Erickson. Amsterdam: Rodopi, 1979.

_____. *Plato: An Introduction.* Translated by H. Meyerhoff. New York: Harper & Row (Harper Torchbooks), 1958.

Gelb, I. J., *A Study of Writing*, revised ed. Chicago and London: University of Chicago Press, 1974.

Gercke, A. "Die alte τέχνη ῥητορική und ihre Gegner." *Hermes*, 32 (1897): 341–381.

Gold, Barbara K. *Literary Patronage in Greece and Rome.* Chapel Hill and London: The University of North Carolina Press, 1987.

Gomperz, Heinrich. *Sophistik und Rhetorik.* Stuttgart: B. G. Teubner Verlagsgesellschaft, 1965 (reprint of 1912 ed.).

Gomperz, Theodor. *Griechische Denker: Eine Geschichte der Antiken Philosophie.* Leipzig: Veit & Comp., 1896–1909.

Grant, Michael. *The Visible Past: Greek and Roman History from Archaeology, 1960–1990.* New York: Charles Scribner's Sons, 1990.

Griffith, G. T. "The Greek Historians." In *Fifty Years (and Twelve) of Classical Scholarship*, 2nd ed., edited by Maurice Platnauer. Oxford: Basil Blackwell, 1968.

Grimaldi, William M. A., S. J. *Aristotle, Rhetoric I: A Commentary.* New York: Fordham University Press, 1980.

Gronbeck, Bruce. "Gorgias on Rhetoric and Poetic: A Rehabilitation," *Southern Speech Communication Journal*, 38 (1972): 27–38.

Guido, Margaret. *Sicily: An Archaeological Guide.* London: Faber and Faber Limited, 1967.

Guthrie, W. K. C. *A History of Greek Philosophy*, Vol. 2. Cambridge: Cambridge University Press, 1965.

_____. *The Sophists*. Cambridge: Cambridge University Press, 1971.

Hammond, N. G. L. "The Campaign and Battle of Marathon." *Journal of Hellenic Studies*, 88 (1968): 13–57.

Hargis, Donald E. "The Rhapsode." *Quarterly Journal of Speech*, 56 (1970): 388–397.

_____. "Socrates and the Rhapsode: Plato's *Ion*." In *Studies in Interpretation*, vol. 2, edited by Esther M. Doyle and Virginia Hastings Floyd. Amsterdam: Rodopi, 1977.

Havelock, Eric A. *The Literate Revolution in Greece and Its Cultural Consequences*. Princeton, NJ: Princeton University Press, 1982.

_____. *Preface to Plato*. Cambridge, MA: Harvard University Press, 1963 (reprint 1982).

Hayman, Henry. "On Early Greek Written Literature." *Journal of Philology*, 8 (1879): 144 ff.

Hinks, D. A. G. "Tisias and Corax and the Invention of Rhetoric." *Classical Quarterly*, 34 (April 1940): 61–69.

_____. "Tria Genera Causarum." Classical Quarterly, 30 (1936): 170–176.

Hubbell, Harry M. "The Rhetoric of Philodemus." *Transactions of the Connecticut Academy of Arts and Sciences*, 23 (1920): 364–382.

Hudson-Williams, H. Ll. "Greek Orators and Rhetoric." In *Fifty Years (and Twelve) of Classical Scholarship*, edited by Maurice Platnauer. Oxford: Basil Blackwell, 1968.

Hunt, Everett Lee. "Plato and Aristotle on Rhetoric and Rhetoricians." In *Historical Studies of Rhetoric and Rhetoricians*, edited by Raymond F. Howes. Ithaca, NY: Cornell University Press, 1961.

Hyland, Drew A. (1968). "Why Plato Wrote Dialogues." *Philosophy and Rhetoric*, 1 (1968): 38–50.

Immerwahr, Henry R. *Form and Thought in Herodotus*. Cleveland, OH: Press of Western Reserve University, 1966.

Jacoby, Felix. Atthis: *The Local Chroniclers of Ancient Athens*. Oxford: Clarendon Press, 1949.

Jaeger, Werner. *Paideia: The Ideals of Greek Culture*, three vols., translated by Gilbert Highet. New York: Oxford University Press, 1943–1945.

_____. "The Rhetoric of Isocrates and Its Cultural Ideal." In *Essays on the Rhetoric of the Western World*, edited by Edward P. J. Corbett, James L. Golden, and Goodwin F. Berquist. Dubuque, IA: Kendall/Hunt Publishing Company, 1990.

Jarratt, Susan C. *Rereading the Sophists: Classical Rhetoric Refigured*. Carbondale and Edwardsville: Southern Illinois University Press, 1991.

Jebb, Richard C. *The Attic Orators from Antiphon to Isaeos*, two vols. New York: Russell and Russell, 1962.

Jesperson, Otto. *Language: Its Nature, Development and Origin.* London: George Allen and Unwin Ltd., 1964.

Johnson, R. "Isocrates' Method of Teaching." *American Journal of Philology,* 80 (1959): 25–36.

Johnstone, Henry W., Jr. *Validity and Rhetoric in Philosophical Argument: An Outlook in Transition.* University Park, PA: The Dialogue Press of Man & World, 1978.

Kauffman, Charles. "Enactment as Argument in the *Gorgias.*" *Philosophy and Rhetoric,* 12 (1979): 114–129.

Kaufer, David S. "The Influence of Plato's Developing Psychology on His Views of Rhetoric." *Quarterly Journal of Speech,* 64 (1978): 63–78.

Kenyon, Frederic George and Colin Henderson. "Books, Greek and Latin." In *The Oxford Classical Dictionary.* 2nd ed. N. G. L. Hammond and H. H. Scullard. Oxford: Clarendon Press, 1970.

Kennedy, George A. "The Ancient Dispute Over Rhetoric in Homer." *American Journal of Philology,* 78 (1957): 23–35.

_____. *Aristotle, On Rhetoric: A Theory of Civic Discourse; Newly Translated with Introduction, Notes, and Appendixes.* New York and Oxford: Oxford University Press, 1991.

_____. *The Art of Persuasion in Greece.* Princeton: Princeton, NJ: University Press, 1963.

_____. *Classical Rhetoric and Its Christian and Secular Tradition from Ancient to Modern Times.* Chapel Hill: The University of North Carolina Press, 1980.

_____. "The Earliest Rhetorical Handbooks." *American Journal of Philology,* 80 (1959): 169–178.

_____. "Later Greek Philosophy and Rhetoric." *Philosophy and Rhetoric,* 13 (Summer 1980): 181–197.

_____. "Review Article: The Present State of the Study of Ancient Rhetoric." *Classical Philology,* 70 (1975): 278–282.

Kerferd, G. B. "Gorgias on Nature or That Which is Not." *Phronesis,* 1 (1955): 3–25.

_____. *The Sophistic Movement.* Cambridge: Cambridge University Press, 1981.

Kindstrand, Jan Fredrik. *Homer in der Zweiten Sophistik: Studien zu der Homerlekture und dem Homerbild bei Dion von Prusa, Maximos von Tyros und Ailios Aristeides.* Acta Universitatis, Upsaliensis Studia Graeca Upsaliensia, 7, edited by Jonas Palm. Uppsala, Stockholm: Almqvist & Wiksell, 1973.

Kirk, G. S. *Homer and the Epic.* Cambridge: Cambridge University Press, 1965.

_____. *Homer and the Oral Tradition.* Cambridge: Cambridge University Press, 1976.

_____. *The Songs of Homer.* Cambridge: Cambridge University Press, 1962.

Kirk, G. S. and J. E. Raven. *The Presocratic Philosophers: A Critical History with a Selection of Texts*. Cambridge: Cambridge University Press, 1973.

Kleinknecht, Hermann. "Herodot und Athen." *Hermes*, 75 (1940): 241–264.

Kustas, George L. *Studies in Byzantine Rhetoric*. Thessaloniki: Patriarxikon Iaryma Paterikon Meleton, 1973.

Lamb, W. R. M., trans. *Plato: Laches, Protagoras, Meno, Euthydemus*. The Loeb Classical Library. Cambridge: Harvard University Press, 1967.

Langer, Susanne K. *Philosophy in a New Key: A Study in the Symbolism of Reason, Rite and Art*, third ed. Cambridge: Harvard University Press, 1976.

Lateiner, Donald. *The Historical Method of Herodotus*. Toronto: University of Toronto Press, 1989.

Lentz, Tony M. *Orality and Literacy in Hellenic Greece*. Carbondale: Southern Illinois University Press, 1989.

Lesky, Albin. *A History of Greek Literature*, translated by James Willis and Cornelis de Heer. New York: Thomas Y. Crowell, 1966.

Levi, Albert William. "Philosophy as Literature: The Dialogue." *Philosophy and Rhetoric*, 9 (1976): 1–20, 24–26.

Levi, Adolfo. "Logos." *Studi su Gorgia* (1941): 24–26. Cited in Mario Untersteiner, *The Sophists*, 155, ns. 83–84.

Liddell, George and Robert Scott, eds. *A Greek-English Lexicon*. Revised by Henry Stuart Jones et al. Oxford: Clarendon Press, 1968.

Loenen, Johannes H. M. M. *Parmenides, Melissus, Gorgias: A Reinterpretation of Eleatic Philosophy*. Assen, The Netherlands: Royal VanGorcum Ltd., 1959.

Lord, Albert B. *The Singer of Tales*. New York: Atheneum, 1976.

Maas, Paul. *Greek Metre*, translated by Hugh Lloyd-Jones. Oxford: Clarendon Press, 1972.

Maidment, K. J. *Minor Attic Orators, I: Antiphon, Andocides*. The Loeb Classical Library. London: William Heinemann, 1968.

Martin, Josef. *Antike Rhetorik: Technik und Methode*. Munchen: C. H. Beck'sche Verlagsbuchhandlung, 1974.

Meyer, Michel. "Dialectic and Questioning: Socrates and Plato." *American Philosophical Quarterly*, 17 (1980): 281–289.

———. "The Nature of Problematic Knowledge." In *Questions and Questioning*, edited by M. Meyer. Berlin and New York: Walter de Gruyter, 1988.

Miller, Molly. *The Sicilian Colony Dates: Studies in Chronography, I*. Albany: State University of New York Press, 1970.

Morrison, J. S. "The Place of Protagoras in Athenian Public Life (460–415 B.C.)." *Classical Quarterly*, 35 (April 1941): 1–16.

Mure, William. *A Critical History of the Language and Literature of Ancient Greece*, vol 4. London: Longman, Brown, Green & Longmans, 1853.

Murphy, James J. "Corax, Tisias, and the 'Invention' of Rhetoric." In *A Synoptic History of Classical Rhetoric*, edited by James J. Murphy. New York: Random House, 1972.

Murray, James S. "Disputation, Deception and Dialectic: Plato on the True Rhetoric (*Phaedrus* 261–266)." *Philosophy and Rhetoric*, 21 (1988): 279–289.

Mutschmann, Hermann. "Die alteste Definition der Rhetorik." *Hermes*, 53 (1918): 440–443.

Myres, John L. *Herodotus: The Father of History*. Oxford: Clarendon Press, 1953.

Navarre, Octave Lucien Louis. *Essai sur la rhétorique grecque avant Aristote*. Paris: Hachette, 1900.

Norden, Eduard. *Die Antike Kuntsprosa*, two vols. Stuttgart: B. G. Teubner, 1909, 1918, 1974.

North, Helen F. *Sophrosyne: Self-Knowledge and Self-Restraint in Greek Literature*. Ithaca, NY: Cornell University Press, 1966.

_____ "Swimming Upside Down in the Wrong Direction: Plato's Criticism of Sophistic Rhetoric on Technical and Stylistic Grounds." ΠΑΡΑΔΟΣΙΣ, 32 (1976): 11–29.

Ong, Walter J., S.J. *Orality and Literacy: The Technologizing of the Word*. New York: Methuen, 1982.

Oxford Classical Dictionary (OCD). Ed. N. G. L. Hammond and H. H. Scullard, 2nd ed. Oxford: Clarendon Press, 1970.

Palmer, L. R. *The Greek Language*. Atlantic Highlands, NJ: Humanities Press, Inc. (Faber & Faber), 1980.

Parry, Adam, ed. *The Making of Homeric Verse: The Collected Papers of Milman Parry*. Oxford: Clarendon Press, 1971.

Parry, Milman. *L'Épithète traditionnelle dans Homère*. Paris: Société Éditrice Les Belles Lettres, 1928.

_____. "Studies in the Epic Technique of Oral Verse-Making: Ii. The Homeric Language as the Language of Oral Poetry." *Harvard Studies in Classical Philology*, 43 (1932), 1–50.

Patzer, Harald. "Ραψῳδός." *Hermes*, 80 (1952): 314–325.

Pavese, Carolo Odo. *Studi Sulla Tradizione Epica Rapsodia*. Roma: Edizioni dell'Ateneo, 1974.

Peabody, Berkley. *The Winged Word: A Study in the Technique of Ancient Greek Oral Composition as Seen Principally through Hesiod's Works and Days*. Albany: State University of New York Press, 1975.

Pearson, Lionel. *Early Ionian Historians*. Oxford: Clarendon Press, 1939.

Perelman, Chaim. *The Realm of Rhetoric*. Notre Dame: University of Notre Dame Press, 1982.

Perelman, Chaim and L. Olbrechts-Tyteca. *The New Rhetoric: A Treatise on Argumentation*. Trans. John Wilkinson and Purcell Weaver. Notre Dame: University of Notre Dame Press, 1971.

Perry, Ben Edwin. "The Early Greek Capacity for Viewing Things Separately." *Transactions of the American Philological Association,* 68 (1937): 410–418.

Petracos, Basil Chr. *The Amphiareion of Oropos.* Athens: Esperos Editions, 1974.

Pfeiffer, Rudolf. *History of Classical Scholarship: From the Beginnings to the End of the Hellenistic Age.* Oxford: Clarendon Press, 1971.

Pope, Maurice. *The Story of Archaeological Decipherment: From Egyptian Hieroglyphs to Linear B.* New York: Charles Scribner's Sons, 1975.

Pucci, Pietro. *Hesiod and the Language of Poetry.* Baltimore and London: Johns Hopkins University Press, 1977.

Quimby, Rollin W. "The Growth of Plato's Perception of Rhetoric." *Philosophy and Rhetoric,* 7 (1974): 71–79.

Radermacher, Ludwig. "Anfange der Charakterkunde bei den Griechen." *Symbolae Osloensis,* 19–24, fasc. 27 (1949).

Ranulf, Svend. *The Jealousy of the Gods and Criminal Law at Athens,* vol. 1. London: Williams and Norgate, 1933.

Real-Encyclopädie der klassischen Altertumswissenschaft, edited by A. Pauly, G. Wissowa, and Wilhelm Kroll. "Korax," vol. 11, colms. 1378–1381 (Lammert); "Teisias," vol. 5a (suppl.), part 1, colms. 138–149 (K. Mittelhaus, Willy Stegemann and Hans Nachod); "Rhetorik, (Korax und Teisias)," vol 7 (suppl.), colms. 1041–1042 (W. Kroll). Stuttgart: J. B. Metzlersche Verlangsbuchhandlung, 1922, 1934, 1940.

Reale, Giovanni. *The Concept of First Philosophy and the Unity of the Metaphysics of Aristotle,* edited and translated by John R. Catan. Albany: State University of New York Press, 1980.

Renault, Mary. *The Praise Singer.* New York: Pantheon Books, 1978.

Rendall, Steven. "Dialogue, Philosophy, and Rhetoric: The Example of Plato's *Gorgias.*" *Philosophy and Rhetoric,* 10 (1977): 164–179.

Roberts, W. Rhys. "The New Rhetorical Fragment (*Oxyrhynchus Papyri,* Part III., pp. 27–30) in Relation to the Sicilian Rhetoric of Corax and Tisias." *Classical Review,* 18 (February 1904): 18–21.

Rosenmeyer, Thomas G. "Gorgias, Aeschylus and '*Apate.*'" *American Journal of Philology,* 76 (1955): 225–260.

Schiappa, Edward. *Protagoras and Logos: A Study in Greek Philosophy and Rhetoric.* Columbia: University of South Carolina Press, 1991.

Segal, Charles P. "Gorgias and the Psychology of the Logos." *Harvard Studies in Classical Philology,* 66 (1962): 99–155.

Selfe, Lois S. "Rhetoric and *Phronesis*: The Aristotelian Ideal." *Philosophy and Rhetoric,* 12 (1979), 130–145.

Sesonske, Alexander. "To Make the Weaker Argument Defeat the Stronger." In *Plato: True and Sophistic Rhetoric,* edited by K. V. Erickson. Amsterdam: Rodopi, 1979.

Skousgaard, Stephen. "Genuine Speech vs. Chatter: A Socratic Problematic." In *Plato: True and Sophistic Rhetoric*, edited by K. V. Erickson. Amsterdam: Rodopi, 1979.

Smith, Bromley. "Corax and Probability." Quarterly Journal of Speech, 7 (February 1921): 13–42.

_____. "Gorgias: A Study in Oratorical Style." Quarterly Journal of Speech, 7 (November 1921): 335–359.

Solmsen, Friedrich. "The Aristotelian Tradition in Ancient Rhetoric." American Journal of Philology, 62 (1941): 35–50, 169–190. Reprinted in *Aristotle: The Classical Heritage of Rhetoric*, 278–309, edited by Keith V. Erickson. Metuchen, NJ: The Scarecrow Press, 1974.

_____. "The 'Gift' of Speech in Homer and Hesiod." *Transactions of the American Philological Association*, 85 (1954): 1–15.

Solmsen, L. "Speeches in Herodotus' Account of the Battle of Plataea." *Classical Philology*, 39 (1944): 241–253.

_____. "Speeches in Herodotus' Account of the Ionian Revolt." *American Journal of Philology*, 64 (1943): 194–207.

Stanford, W. B. *The Sound of Greek: Studies in the Greek Theory and Practice of Euphony*. Berkeley: University of California Press, 1967.

Starr, Chester. *The Awakening of the Greek Historical Spirit*. New York: Knopf, 1968.

Stewart, Donald C. "The Continuing Relevance of Plato's *Phaedrus*." In *Essays on Classical Rhetoric and Modern Discourse*, edited by R. J. Connors, L. S. Ede, and A. Lunsford. Carbondale: Southern Illinois University Press, 1984.

Ullman, Berthold Louis. *Ancient Writing and its Influence*. Cambridge: The MIT Press, 1969.

Untersteiner, Mario. *The Sophists*, translated by Kathleen Freeman. Oxford: Basil Blackwell, 1954.

Vanderpool, Eugene. "The Deme of Marathon and the Herakleion." *American Journal of Archaeology*, 70 (1966), 319–323.

_____. "A Monument to the Battle of Marathon." *Hesperia*, 35 (1966): 93–106.

Vernant, Jean-Pierre. *The Origins of Greek Thought*. Ithaca, NY: Cornell University Press, 1982.

Verrall, A. W. "Korax and Tisias." *Journal of Philology*, 9 (1880): 197–210.

Vickers, Brian. *In Defence of Rhetoric*. Oxford: Oxford University Press, 1988.

Welch, Kathleen Ethel. *The Contemporary Reception of Classical Rhetoric: Appropriations of Ancient Discourse*. Hillsdale, NJ: Lawrence Earlbaum Associates, 1990.

_____. "The Platonic Paradox: Plato's Rhetoric in Contemporary Rhetoric and Composition Studies." *Written Communication*, 5 (1988): 3–21.

Welch, Kathleen Ethel. "Writing Instruction in Ancient Athens After 450 B.C." *A Short History of Writing Instruction: From Ancient Greece to Twentieth-Century America*, edited by James J. Murphy. Davis, CA: Hermagoras Press, 1990.

Welles, C. B. *Royal Correspondence in the Hellenistic Period. A Study in Greek Epigraphy*. Chicago: Ares Publishers, 1974.

West, Martin Litchfield. "Homeridae" and "Rhapsodes." In *The Oxford Classical Dictionary*, 2nd ed., edited by N. G. L. Hammond and H. H. Scullard. Oxford: Clarendon Press, 1970.

Wilcox, Stanley. "Corax and the Prolegomena." *American Journal of Philology*, 64 (January 1943) 1–23.

_____. "Isocrates' Fellow-Rhetoricians." *American Journal of Philology*, 66 (1945): 171--186.

_____. "The Scope of Early Rhetorical Instruction." *Harvard Studies in Classical Philology*, 53 (1942): 121–155.

Woodhead, A. G. *The Greeks in the West*. New York: Frederick A. Praeger Publisher, 1962.

Yates, Frances A. *The Art of Memory*. Chicago: University of Chicago Press, 1966.

Index